Praise for Mina Irfan and Lady Balls

"Mina Irfan's work is the High Value Woman's bible. Her insightful and inspiring words have healed our feminine nature in ways that allow us to show up in life happier, richer, prettier, and more confident. She has given us the blueprint on how to not only show up as a top 1% woman, but also do the inner work." - Lyndosha Jamison, Esq. Attorney and host of Manifest with Lyndosha (YouTube Channel)

"I've worked with dozens of life coaches, relationship coaches, business coaches, and mentors, but there's only one Mina Irfan. She is changing women's lives worldwide. Before working with Mina I was lonely, depressed, overworked, struggling financially, and stuck in a career I didn't desire. Fast forward 1 year later, I've been swept off my feet by a masculine provider, I'm a thriving entrepreneur, and have completely transformed my life. She is the inspiration and teacher you've been looking for." - JoAnna Life, Health, and Fitness Coach @joannajoi

"Working with Mina has changed my life. Mina is so uniquely able to see right through to the scars, conditioning, and self-limiting beliefs that I and so many women need help to overcome. She relentlessly guided me to the pure feminine energy of my soul. She inspired me to nourish my worthiness and see that I already had the permission to achieve and live the life of my dreams. Love you Mina!" - Goddess AngelRose is a Feminine Energy Life Consultant and intuitive Human Design Projector, devoted to helping high-end, high-achieving women who desire to elevate and design their dream life. Aligned Feminine Embodiment. www.afe.life www.YouTube.com/@afelife/

"Raw. Juicy. Sexy. Honest. Mina's material is the transformation you've been waiting for. If you're giddy AND nervous, consider that your green light. Happy activating." - Eleanor David, The Conversationalist, https://eleanordavid.substack.com/

"Mina effortlessly weaves together profound concepts in tangible form. She demonstrates that we really can have it ALL by cultivating our inner world. Her raw approach is authentic and refreshing. She is a true embodiment of the divine feminine. Absolutely life changing!" - Nadine Desormeau, MSOM, L.Ac.

"To reduce Mina's work into a tiny paragraph would be doing us all a disservice. Her wisdom combined with her genuine embodiment has altered my life in immeasurable ways, and that is truly an understatement. Mina has been pivotal in revealing my true me to me. She perfected the art of tough love with matronly love in beautiful harmony.

I must warn you, however, if you read this book, you had better be ready to embark on some deeply transformative changes in your life. If you are willing to do the work, you will see massive quantum shifts. And I personally promise that it'll be worth it. Make the investment in yourself and read this for you, for your future, and for our future generations. With eternal gratitude." - Stef Schiel-James ..SoMoS..

"Today, I feel unstoppable & fully embodied in my femininity!!! I learned to listen to & trust myself even when it's contrary to what everyone else thinks or believes. To look at me now, you would never have believed anything was broken but I started my TUG journey with a shattered soul.

Since beginning the practices of TUG, I have been to every in-person intensive, purchased the University Bundle & everything else TUG offers. To sit at the feet of wisdom, learn & embody it in this moment is priceless. We hear of great teachers of old & wonder what it would have been like to sit at their feet & learn. I don't have to wonder, I get to experience Mina as a spiritual thought leader in my lifetime & that is priceless.

I found Mina while searching for answers to fix my broken heart, life, soul, family & misaligned purpose. I relocated to America under false claims & was exploited my first few years. All the horror stories you hear in exploitation were my reality.

Despite being out of harm's way, my life was a landmine of triggers, traumas, overstepped boundaries, entitled relationship & unexplainable life events. In Spite of my landmine life, my life's purpose kept showing up & I couldn't make sense of it. Intuitively, I felt like I had met my therapy, depression meds, anxiety meds & church cap.

I started searching for holistic & spiritual answers. Within months of turning my back on everything I knew & believed, I found Mina's work. I implemented what I learned, followed up on every resource she shared. Now, I am living my best life off medication & fully in my purpose. Thank you Mina!" - Emalia Denoon, www.SpiritualAndCoachable.com

"Mina evolves at the speed of light. Watching Mina evolve over the years has been one of the most inspirational experiences I've encountered and it has had massive ripple effects in my life. Talk about true embodiment! She doesn't just walk the walk and talk the talk, she lives it every single day. Her teachings about femininity, marriage, money, inner work and God are all deeply rooted in her actual life experiences from a cultural, academic and spiritual perspective which make them truly powerful and life changing for women all around the world." - Ayleen Nazario (AyleenNazario.com)

"Mina is the teacher your soul craves. She doesn't just tell you what to do from her expertise, but like a lighthouse, she also shines so YOU can find your own way home. If she's the light, this book is the map that will wake you up to how to listen to your inner knowing and live your most fulfilling life no matter what. Self help and inner work are a lifelong process, but if you're ready to stop feeling like a project, and actually make leaps and bounds in your growth...look no further than here. This is the best and last transformation teacher you will need and can continually come back to." - Tsika.

"Mina expertly weaves a big-picture view of all the sciences through a very heart-centered, spiritual, feminine frame of reference to help us understand the self. From a place of having done the work, made the mistakes, experienced the trauma, discovered how to heal AND exponentially thrive, she passionately guides you on a deep dive to experiencing YOUR inner knowing.

It's rarc to find such vast knowledge connected across multiple fields of discipline, yet Mina effortlessly combines wisdom of thousands of years of science and spirituality in a practical way. Be prepared for endless inspiration on your journey!" - Erin Pech, Founder, Meadowbelle Jewelry

"Mina Irfan's work, courses and embodiment have quite profoundly altered the entire course of my life. If there was a stage before "Basic Babe", then I was in it. Prior to finding her work I was a self-help junkie for 15 years, reading countless articles online on "How to change your life" yet not being able to, on the verge of divorce, suffering numerous health problems, crippling social anxiety, and to put it quite plainly, a doormat. With unwavering faith, I dove heart-first into her work and manifested my soul's deepest desires that I didn't know were possible or even that I desired it at all including: a home, health, a pain-free birth, a daughter, and now my own business and so much more. Her inner work has so elegantly transformed me into the beautiful feminine woman that I am today with the deepest appreciation for my masculine containers as well. Mina is a true gem, genuine to her core, and the greatest testament of inner work that I have known. I have 100% faith that anything with her name on it holds deep truths and activations. Thank you, Mina, for marrying my spirit to my human and for being the bright light in the universe that has helped myself and countless others have the courage to radiate theirs." - Row Ahmed, Weight Loss Coach @DefaultAbundance

"Since I found Mina's work a few years ago and from the very first video the content has blown my mind and changed the way I see and live my life so much. Not only it opens my mind to new knowledge but it has also helped me reconnect with my own wisdom and intuition. It has helped me in the practical ways of structuring life like money, household, relationships, etc., but also to reconnect with myself, with my spirituality and connection to the Universe and God and everything in between. If you think it sounds too good to be true you wait for it, you haven't seen anything yet. Getting to Mina's field has unravel grids and aspects of life I never had access to before, they probably were there all along but I just got to know them once my field opened to them, and this was that door to me. I manifested so much abundance in my life, I changed the country I live in, the people I relate to and re-discovered my relationship with God. I cannot stretch in words how much I recommend Mina's work even before the book was published and before knowing what it was going to be about I knew I was going to buy it and read it all. As I have done before with her online courses and I've never been disappointed in doing so. I can assure you that it doesn't matter what you are going through now you will always hear and get what you need in the moment. If you are here reading this right now for a reason, don't let the opportunity of getting the answers you were asking pass you by. I will always be grateful for the learnings I got from Mina Irfan." - Paula Pazmiño

Lady Balls

How to Be Savagely Successful in a World Addicted to Suffering

Mina Irfan

TheUniverseGuru LLC
Houston, Texas

DISCLAIMER: The information is this book is intended for educational and entertainment purposes only. This book is not intended to be a substitute for the legal, medical, psychological, or financial advice of professionals. The author or publisher are not offering professional services advice.

The author and publisher assume no responsibility for your actions and specifically disclaim responsibility for any liability, loss, risk, or any physical, psychological, emotional, financial, or commercial damages, personal or otherwise, which is incurred as a consequence, directly or indirectly, of the use and application of any of the contents of this book.

Lady Balls\Mina Irfan - 1st ed.

ISBN: 979-8-9890423-0-2 (Paperback)
ISBN: 979-8-9890423-2-6 (Ebook)
ISBN: 979-8-9890423-8-8 (Hardback)

To 7 generations back and 7 generations forward.

For Sheena and Alina.

For us.

CONTENTS

FOREWORD

By Shahrzad Parandeh, Life and Relationship Mentor, and the Creator of The Fully Adored and The Masterpiece Woman brand!

In 2017, many significant things happened in my life. I was finally engaged to the man of my dreams, started my coaching business, left my corporate job, and I will confidently put meeting Mina in that same category. Divine intervened to show me everything I needed to know when it came to breaking through my limitations and to live the life that my heart desired!

As a woman from Iran, I had grown up with a lot of Eastern values, but as we moved to Canada when I turned 14, I felt a lot of confusion about what I believed was possible for me as a woman. At first, as a rebellious teenager, I immediately felt "free," believing I could be and do anything that was available to boys. Although my parents did their best to stop me from throwing away the values they raised me with when it came to my relationship with the opposite sex, I went about it my own way. It took me 16 years of dating according to what is deemed normal in Western culture, having my heart shattered and my power taken away, until I came back to my roots and realized that what I used to consider a limitation was actually the truest form of honor for the feminine and the key to success in a romantic relationship.

Now, don't get me wrong: growing up in Canada also gave me a world of possibilities to excel in my education. I was able to develop my masculine energy as I earned my Master's Degree in Civil Engineering and pursued a career that allowed me to travel to over 20 countries on every continent. Travel, I must say, was one of the biggest catalysts for my growth, both as a woman and as a spiritual being.

But when it came to the passage to womanhood and starting a family, I was in constant battle within myself and with men until I started to approach and embody my quest to find my forever man through practices rooted in Eastern culture.

While I was doing my best to blend what I had learned from my culture with the best parts of the Western world to be successful in both my relationship and coaching career, the Divine intervened, as I mentioned, and there she was: Mina Irfan, The Universe Guru!

Up until the point of finding Mina, I felt like an oddball. Sure, there were many incredible mentors out there from whom I had learned, but a role model who was raised with similar values, had the healthiest and most beautiful marriage, and ran a thriving coaching business where she actually taught the very things I believe are the keys to the heaven of being a woman who is and has it all, I hadn't seen anyone like that before... Finding Mina shifted my paradigm forever!

Not only did Mina quickly become my friend, but I had to take her courses and have her as my teacher!

Year after year, I have the privilege to witness her grow at an inexplicable speed, as she gives so much value through her ever-flourishing YouTube channel and her courses. Her work is the masterful blend of the best of both Eastern and Western worlds.

Mina and her divine work are what all women need in our world.

When she told me she was writing this book, I immediately knew that a masterpiece was about to be born, and I want to sincerely congratulate you because what you're holding in your hands has the potential to radically change the course of your life.

I want to invite you to keep an open mind if what you desire is to have it all! This book is your sacred passage to womanhood, to having the relationship of your dreams, the peaceful life - mind - home, the sacred family, the success, wealth beyond your wildest dreams, and more!

It was about time that somebody told us the truth as it is, and Mina has the Lady Balls to do exactly that!

It's time to savagely claim what's yours and let go of suffering, babe! You deserve it!

Shahrzad Parandeh, Life and Relationship Mentor, and the Creator of The Fully Adored and The Masterpiece Woman brand!

INTRODUCTION

When this book first started creating itself through me, the downloads were coming through in non-linear blocks, images, and stories. I would get a paragraph in Chapter Seven, and then a section of Chapter Two would follow. This made complete sense to the non-linear nature of my metaphysical self. However, it was driving my human self crazy!

Mildly annoyed, I went to my husband for support. "*Why can't I write this book in a linear fashion like I did my first book?*"

"*Do you know how movies are made?*" he asked me.

"*No, not really,*" I replied.

"*Movies are filmed out of sequence in small shots. Depending on the schedules of the actors, and the seasons they need for the shots, and various other aspects, they film the scenes in the sequence they can at the moment. Regardless of its place in the movie,*" he explained. "*So, the ending shots may be the first shots to be filmed, and then the beginning, followed by the middle shots and so forth until the whole movie is complete.*"

"*You have to see your book in three timelines,*" he continued. "*There are the downloads you are getting, out of linear sync like shots in a movie. Then there is timeline two, which is your actual transformation story. How you overcame your past and became successful using inner work. And then there is a third timeline, where you start telling the story in the book."*

My mind was already blown.

He continued to explain that most movies, like my book, don't start at the beginning of the actual timeline. They start somewhere in the middle and then flash backwards and forward as needed. It was true! Most of the movies I loved just threw the viewer into the action at any point in the timeline! And told the story from that perspective, moving back and forth in time as needed. Movies, just like all of the best stories ever told, were non-linear!

And in that moment, God had used my husband to speak to me. It suddenly all made sense. My first book, *Contained in Love* (Second Edition) started the timeline from my journey after marrying Irfan and settling into my new role as a wife and mother. That story timeline ended in 2016 when that book was published. I recently released the second edition adding in updates to each chapter from my current viewpoint.

So much has happened since 2016 that you would think I have started a completely new life since that book was published. The book you hold in your hands serves as both a how to guide and a chronicle of the savage awakening of one badass woman.

Oceans of love,

Mina Irfan

August 24, 2023

CHAPTER *One*
YOUR DESIRES ARE NOT PROBLEMS

"*If I had a million dollars, I would invest it, live off the interest and read all day.*" These words were uttered by my writing professor at Northwestern University a little more than two decades ago. I didn't particularly like the class or this particular professor. It was my least favorite class mainly because of her rude, irritated attitude. It was obvious to all of us that our professor hated her job. She once mentioned only working because her husband's job didn't provide health insurance. Years earlier, I was encouraged by my 7th grade teacher to "continue writing" after winning the Young Author's Award for the state of Illinois. At this time in my life, I never saw myself as a writer, or anything else for that matter. But I had given her my word and so here I was, sitting in a hot, sticky classroom in July, taking a writing class.

And then those paradigm shifting words, casually uttered from her, changed my life. That is why I ended up in her class, I thought. To hear those exact words. I didn't hear the rest of what she said or why she was talking about having a million dollars in the first place. I was in sheer intoxication from the desire she had just invoked in me.

Wait, you can invest money and live off of it and read all day?

And never have to deal with people?

How come no one ever told me this before!!

What else don't I know about money?

My brain was going in all sorts of directions. Question after question was popping up with excitement! She had just described my dream life. My introverted soul was beaming with possibilities. I had no idea you could do that kind of stuff with money. It was decided at that moment, I was going to have a million dollars and stay home to read all day. That day one of the deepest desires of my heart was summoned and it changed the course of my entire life. More than the money, I wanted a life of peace and ease. The money was my gateway into my dream lifestyle.

Divine Desires

It would be about 12 years from that exact day before I actually had a million dollars. However, a part of my desire came true only about 8 years later when I got married and my husband retired me at the age of 28. I suddenly had time to sit and read as many books as I wanted. I used that time very wisely and dived into deep inner work.

I take my desires as proof that God has approved and created that potential timeline for me already.

From there I have two options: I can either accept the assignment or leave it by doubting or questioning it. Be honest, would you have considered my desire for a million dollars invested to just read all day as an actual possibility in your life? Or would you have questioned the hell out of the how and when?

Your Desires are Divine Directions to a different location in time/space where something new and different is available for you. God has already decided and is showing you a glimpse of a different location in time/space. You are summoned to something bigger and greater, a new possibility awaits. Unlike what we have been told to believe, our desires are not greedy, dirty, or unrealistic. Your desires are not problems that need to be figured out. You just have to accept it as a possible reality in existence in an alternative timeline and move accordingly. I would never question a preview that God was already showing me. If there is a preview, the movie already exists.

Desires are the gateway to the downloads from the Divine Feminine herself. As you will learn in this book, you are the human manifestation of Divine Feminine energy itself. Living in a world that values masculine energy over feminine energy, our desires are often made wrong. We judge them as too much, too greedy, or too whatever.

I do not blame men. They have been conditioned to put aside their own desires for the betterment of society. To hunt, provide, protect. Even go to war if needed. The men who woke up in the hunter-gatherer days and refused to go hunt because they "didn't feel like it" died. We are not their descendants.

Men evolved to put aside their own feelings and desires and so that's what they often expect women to do as well. You are not a man. You are a woman. If you are drawn to my work, chances are you are naturally a feminine essence woman who has overly cultivated her masculine side due to one reason or another. More on this later. This first thing we must agree on if you continue reading this book is the fact that men and women are very different. Biologically, physically, mentally, hormonally, and relationally different. Different doesn't mean right or wrong, or one is superior to the other. They simply bring different values to the genetic game we are all playing here momentarily in our limited lifetime.

We have inherited millions of years of programming from our hunter-gatherer ancestors. So, when our father, brother, husband thinks our desires are "too much," they are repeating the script they have been taught. Having desires is often seen as being ungrateful, unhappy, or God forbid, downright greedy. I have seen this pattern in the hundreds of private clients I have served and the tens of thousands of students who have taken my digital courses.

We seem to have this annoyance, irritated energy towards the divine downloads we commonly refer to as desires in the earthly plane. Many of these women get the sacred nudge and instantly go into "problem solving" mode. Either they talk themselves out of the desire or they treat it like this annoying goal they must reach in record time. Usually with a big hefty price tag attached to it, or "some sort of penance to pay".

There is a big difference between desires and goals. Desires are feminine while goals are more masculine. Desires feel good at every point of the journey to our feminine side, even if they don't make sense logically. The million dollars I desired felt so good even before I actually had the money in my bank. Goals give the illusion of something outside of us that we must achieve, work towards, and tick off our to do list. There's nothing wrong with that, but it appeals more to our masculine side. The same million dollars can be savored as a desire of our heart, or set as a goal where we can't rest or have fun until it's reached. One makes you feel good and inspired and the other creates a sense of loss and not enoughness.

Growing up, we didn't have a lot of money. In fact, my mother didn't start making a lot of money until I was already an independent young adult and making my own money. I always had a lot of desires even as a child. My mother, Sheena, used to say, "*Mina wants something from every aisle of every store.*" It's true. I wanted so much, but received messages from those around me that there was never enough.

Today, I honor my desires and see them as the divine creation inspiration as they are. The truth is that the feminine desire is what creates worlds. It's the reason we have civilization. Our cavemen ancestors would have still been living in caves if it wasn't for a cavewoman's desire for something more. To desire is to evolve. Desires, you see, are not meant to be solved, completed, attained, conquered, combated, put out, or any of the other masculine attributes or behaviors we try to throw at them. Desires just are. Little previews from the Divine of what's to come.

The Divine has already decided, hence the preview, or movie trailer is shown to you. The Universe is now waiting on you to DECIDE, to make a decision of free will. Your permission and decision is what the entire thing is hinging on from there. A decision isn't something you declare with your mouth. It's not something you tell a few friends or post on your socials about. Words are cheap; everyone has them. A decision is an internal knowing and agreement to God's plan. You and God got together and aligned. All of YOU is in on this decision. Not just your mouth. Not just your head. Or even your hands and feet. ALL of you! Especially that pesky 95% percent of you we lovingly refer to as the subconscious mind.

That powerful "owning" of my newfound "become a millionaire" desire started that day but didn't actually become reality until about 12 years later. Turns out, I had some inner work to do to truly align and become a match for such a potent desire. Inner Work is the process of elimination. Deconstructing and then reconstructing ourselves to align with our desires. It's the gap between the metaphysical and the manifestation.

I have learned to receive my desires as a preview of what God has planned for me. My job in the process is to simply be God's hands and feet. Listen for those internal nudges and take aligned, quantum action. One way I explain this to my clients is to stay at the desire counter, not the complaint counter. A desire is,

"I would love to have a million dollars invested so I can stay home and read all day."

A complaint is anything other than the original desire. *"Why don't I have a million dollars yet?"*

Or, *"How come the rich get richer while I struggle with getting a promotion?"*

Complaints come with irritated, annoyed, disempowered energy that keeps us in victim mode. Staying at the desire counter keeps us in God's flow. The Divine pings and instructions are much more clearer here. The complaint counter constricts us and puts us in the mental plane. The complaint counter makes us think we have to resolve our desires as if they were problems to be solved! This is an illusion. The mental plane, or your logical mind, is great at looking for perceived threats and warning you about them. It's also great at helping you worry so you can find ways to survive and keep threats at bay. It's not designed to receive divine instructions.

Throughout this book, you will hear the various desires that showed up and how I was divinely led to their manifestations. I have used the process, mindsets, and savagery in this book to manifest all the divine desires of my heart. I believe it is our birthright to have and be it all. This process has been successfully now applied by tens of thousands of women of all ages, backgrounds, nationalities, and religions.

Part of the inner work I had to do on the path to having my desire manifest in the physical reality, was to remove all the obstacles that often showed up—both internally and externally! My first grand manifestation was getting into Northwestern University. No one around me at the time thought I had the grades or brains to actually get in. People were shocked to learn that it was the only school I applied to and got in on the first try as I knew I would. No plan B needed when you know it's been decided. It also made me realize how much I underestimated myself!

In my early 20s, I had a "failed" marriage that blessed me with many lessons and a beautiful baby boy. I use the word failed lightly because I actually don't believe in failure, only God giving me the lessons I need and then rerouting me. I continued my school and launched a successful multiple six figure real estate business during that time as a way to support myself and my son. At 27 I met and married my now husband, Irfan, who proposed in two weeks and retired me from my business after our marriage two months later. After six years of hustling in my real estate business while completing my studies at Northwestern as a single mom, I was pretty burnt out and happy for the change of pace.

Although my husband was not a millionaire at the time, he gave me the opportunity to retire, look after my son, and read all day long. Sometimes the Universe grants our desires in stages and layers. I was perfectly fine with that.

Due to our constant moving and inconsistent lifestyle in my childhood, more on this later, I really desired a paid off house that I owned outright. A few short years after marriage, we finally paid off our home in South Carolina. I then manifested a move to my dream city of Houston, Texas. I always wanted to live in Texas since I was a little girl after visiting my cousins here for a couple of summers.

After moving to Houston, I was diagnosed with rheumatoid arthritis, a brutal autoimmune disease that affects your bones and joints. I refused medication and manifested a full recovery within a few years through lifestyle and nutrition changes. I was now starting to see myself as the manifestation Queen that I was. The new identity was fully formed and owned! You can learn more on my journey in my first book, *Contained in Love.*

At age 33, only a few months before our daughter was born, which was another huge manifestation in our lives, we finally reached our million dollar net worth. A few years later, I manifested a whole romantic transformation in my marriage. My marriage was always good, but I wanted more! After doing some massive inner work, my husband and I developed a more robust, romantic, honeymoon forever type of marriage. I now have the marriage right out of the deepest desires of my heart. I will be sharing how I did that using the principles of polarity with you later in this book.

In 2016, I launched my life coaching business and wrote my first book, now in its second edition, *Contained in Love.* Another desire that I had since winning the Young Author's Award in junior high! In November of 2017, I launched my first digital course, making multiple six figures in my first year. The six figure years quickly turned into six figure months. Every year thereafter, we have been serving more and more people and God has been blessing us with more income rapidly as a result.

I had my first million dollar month in November of 2022, only five years later. Also becoming Thinkific's (the platform where all our courses live) #1 seller for 2022. In the United States, I am the top 1% within the top 1% of earners. My net worth is also in the top 1%. I have also had the pleasure of coaching and mentoring the world's most fabulous top 1% women.

At the time of this writing, I have created over 60 digital courses, hosted over a dozen and a half in-person events, and have impacted tens of thousands of women all over the planet. The transformation testimonials pour in daily and I couldn't be more proud.

I now live in my dream body, which lives in my dream 8600 square foot mansion which was custom designed and previously owned by a famous NBA player. I continue to do my inner work and raise the ceiling as well as the damn floor of what's possible for me and, as a result, all women. To say I have the Midas touch would be an understatement. "*Everything I touch turns to gold*" has been one of my favorite affirmations for years. Turns out this is a skillset that I not only embody, but am also brilliant at activating in other people.

I say all this to not only show you all that can be manifested as a result of our inner work, but also as an embodiment and unapologetic owning and celebration of our feminine successes. And yes, feminine success looks and feels very different from masculine success as you will learn in this book. I don't subscribe to the narrative that we must play small, stay quiet about our achievements or look humble, so as to not offend other people.

Any woman holding the top 1% percent position in any area of her life is a huge accomplishment for all women. Especially considering it hasn't been that long since we were even allowed to have our own careers, bank accounts, and businesses. I have been referred to this four-minute mile by thousands of women and am proud to hold the vision of what's possible for YOU. Any woman's success is every woman's success. Success is not only a birthright, it's also our gift to humanity. And there are infinite amounts of success available to all of us.

God will Never Run Out

We seem to have this belief that if someone else has found success in the area that we desire, then there is suddenly less for us. Or it's suddenly overcrowded or oversaturated. But the truth is that the Universe is not a peasant. Not only is there infinite potential for all of us, but that potential is always growing. Like literally "all that is" is always expanding, ask any quantum physicist.

I am here to tell you that you, too, can have a beautiful life of love, romance, riches, and infinite amounts of pleasure. All the feminine desires of our heart are a necessary component to helping the Universe expand. The Divine Feminine is often referred to as having a bottomless pit of desires and I am here for it! Our desires create worlds! They are the reason men have been getting up and going to hunt or sit in a cubicle for all those generations. Simply to invest in our pleasure.

Affirm: *"My desires and pleasures are my gift to humanity."*

We have all heard and maybe even talked about how God is almighty and has infinite resources. However, I don't think most people believe or truly embody this belief. I do. I believe God is infinite and will never run out of resources. Humans have convinced themselves and each other that there is a finite number of resources. So, if someone else has something that I desire, then there is less or none for me. This couldn't be further from the truth. Do you really think the Universe, God, or Quantum field is that limited?

Physicists speculate that only 5% of creation substance is currently converted to matter. On top of that, that 95% of raw, original source-building material is expanding every day. By growing I don't mean just spreading out, further away, but actually GROWING. This means God is not only infinite, but that infinite creation substance, from which all things are created, is also increasing.

Yes, babe, the Universe is not a peasant, and therefore we shouldn't be either. Quantum physics teaches us that we are all created from the same divine substance. You, me, the stars, and everything else we can see, hold, touch, and basically refer to as "matter." There is an infinite amount of this substance to create from. Unfortunately, our brain can't fully comprehend this, and often tries to create matter from matter instead of going to the raw materials of source. Which is a lot more work and effort! I have trained myself to create and bring my desires into reality from this raw, sacred source substance, instead of existing matter through the ancient concept of Barkat.

Barkat

Barkat is an Islamic concept that is greatly followed in my parent's home country of Pakistan. Think of Barkat as a universal bank account that exponentially compounds whatever you add to it into infinite blessings. All good deeds are multiplied and mirrored back in your life. It is also used to stretch your existing blessings to make them "enough." Something is said to have "Barkat" if it seems to extend beyond its physical quantity and be and last longer than it should.

When I first learned about this concept as a little girl, I started to notice that my extended family members back home were all using it incorrectly. In fact, my parents were also using it in very limited ways. I have no idea why no one else could understand what I could clearly see. I also noticed that even though they all seemed to be using it incorrectly, it still worked in predictable ways. Everyone was using it to stretch the little they had into "enough." Why wasn't anyone using it to manifest overflow or "more than enough," I wondered.

Like all divine laws, Barkat follows your free will and your instructions. The codes you feed it activate the sequence of manifestations in your life. Most of the people around me were using Barkat to Manifest Down. Here are two ways they were doing this. They were manifesting out and down, which is the most peasant way to use Barkat ever!

Manifesting out is when we are running away from a situation that has already been created versus creating what our heart truly desires. This has a very negative energy and we tend to create the "in between a rock and a hard space" type of situation by manifesting in this way. Think of your dominant energy when you are running away from an existing manifestation that you dislike. It will be a lower frequency consciousness which will put you in resonance with other lower vibe solutions. *"I hate this car and want a new one,"* gives off the energy of hate. *"I appreciate this car and would also love that upgraded one over there,"* is a much better way to use Barkat to manifest!

Manifesting down is when you manifest from a position of survival and not from a position of ultimate divine riches. An example of this is asking for just the next month's rent, instead of asking for so much money that you can be in complete overflow and never have to worry about bills ever again. Remember that Barkat flows in any amount or way we tell it to. Why stay in peasant consciousness with our divine desires and asks?

My relatives were always running away from what they had and asking for only a tiny bit more than the poverty they currently had, never really changing their circumstances. Witnessing this as a child, I decided to just ask for more than I even needed and always be in a space of overflow. According to Barkat there are riches written and waiting in everyone's name. It's your divine inheritance. This is where the whole "you were born rich" concept comes from. Your divine right to riches is awaiting your permission and alignment as it can't be unlocked without your free will.

Ways to Increase Barkat in Your Life

Manifest up and in, not down and out: Appreciate what you currently have AND ask for more. Instead of running away from a situation, move towards something amazing and expansive.

Reframe needs into desires: Needs can have a clingy, chasing energy, which doesn't really suit our Divine Feminine nature. Desires feel good and activate our natural creative, intuitive, visualizing abilities.

Become a High Hope person: Believe in God's abundance, not in earthly peasantry. Stop seeing infinite abundance from the limitations of the human mind to activate your most potent desires.

Share your blessings for exponential growth and Barkat in your life: Anything you put out with love in good faith, exponentially compounds your blessings. A song, a book, an affirmation, a dollar, even a smile put out with love can compound into huge blessings of Barkat in your life.

Ways to Decrease Barkat in Your Life

- Complaining about what you currently have.
- Ungratefulness.
- Harming others and in general having bad intentions towards others.
- Earning your living by stealing, robbing, lying, or in any way that harms others.

- Jealousy and envy towards others.
- Being unhygienic and living in a dirty environment.
- Let Source be Your Only Source

People, places, jobs–nothing is your source, except for the actual source, aka God. Sure, God may choose to use certain people, circumstances, or jobs to channel you money and blessings, but this doesn't suddenly make them your source! Anytime I have fallen into the trap of thinking my manifestation has to come from this one place in this exact way, I have delayed my blessings. God has no competition. I had no idea my retirement was going to come from my future husband. I honestly didn't care how it came as long as I got to enjoy the fruits of the manifestation.

Most people focus so much on the how that they miss the part of relishing in their desires and magnetizing it forth. Looking back, there is no way I could have figured out the HOWs of how everything went down in my life even if I wanted to. The things God now chooses to channel blessings into my life didn't even exist when the original desire was planted into my life. The internet that I now use to share my message wasn't even invented yet. YouTube, where I livestream and connect with my audience, didn't exist.

There was no way I could have thought of these things as the "how" to any of my desires when they literally didn't exist. This is why you won't see me wasting time on the "how." I know God will invent, create, lay down the paths to my desires. It's God we are talking about after all. Stop trying to do God's job and literally stay in your own lane.

And as you will see in later chapters of this book, there is no price or penance to pay for your success! Contrary to popular belief, no struggle is required. It honestly doesn't even matter where you started. I literally started at rock bottom and now am at the top 1% of relationship, financial, health, and life success. I wish the same and more for you.

Lesson: Your Desires are Divine Directions to a different location in time/space where something new and different is available for you. They do not need to be problem solved. Use your desires as previews of what's to come.

JOURNAL PROMPTS:

What is the deepest desire of my heart right now? What is the desire I'm not willing to own? What is the desire I am making wrong in some way? What desire am I currently treating like a problem to be solved? What do I truly desire?

Where in my life am I manifesting out and down?

How can I change it to manifesting in and up?

Where in my life am I still manifesting from needs versus desires?

____

____

____

CHAPTER *Two* WOMB WOUNDS

Everything in God's kingdom is created out of the union between masculine and feminine energies. Babies, businesses, art, love, money, and, yes, you and me. Somehow, we have discounted and slowly forgotten this universal truth in the western world. Many other languages still assign masculine and feminine attributions to things. In the English language we simply use the pronoun IT. This is such a shame as masculine and feminine energies are two sides of the same coin. One cannot fully exist and thrive without the other. I have had the pleasure of bringing hundreds of thousands of people back to this wholeness within them.

Both men and women have aspects of the Divine Masculine and Divine Feminine energies inside of them. Masculine energy is the hard, structure setting, linear, rational, accountable, direction and time keeping aspects of us. This is the aspect of us responsible for keeping score, competing, getting ahead, and figuring things out. Without this part holding us together, we don't feel safe. The masculine part in us is very left brain and uses and embodies a more rigid set of formulas, rules, and hierarchies. The masculine is also responsible for creating containment, a sort of holding together, in relationships.

An easy way to remember masculine energy is its ability to take accountability and stand ground in the presence of intensity of emotions and chaos. In any action movie, from any country, the main male lead walks, untouched and unphased, while guns fire around him, bombs blow up behind him, and everyone else runs away in a panic. This is the universal ideal representation of masculine energy in action.

Feminine energy is the soft, warm, non-linear, nurturing, playful, emotional, intuitive, flowy aspects of us. Feminine energy is the more luxurious energy as it is only present in both men and women under certain conditions. Both aspects are necessary parts of our being and need each other to feel whole and happy.

Feminine energy needs masculine energy to exist. Without the providing and protecting of the masculine, the feminine steps into the masculine, herself. As babies, we are mostly in our feminine energy. Think of a baby in her natural feminine being. She flows from being happy, sad, crying, fussy to playful again. She is in touch with her inner emotional world and fully expressing herself. She is able to do this with the feminine nurturing and attunement of her mother and the masculine protection and providing of her father. Take away her parents' masculine structures and feminine presence, and she herself will have to step into her masculine and create coping mechanisms to deal with this immense loss.

Masculine energy is the pillar of outward strength and power, manifested as physical strength due to more testosterone in men. Feminine energy is the deeply mysterious strength and power that comes from inner strength and resilience. They are both very different and yet divinely complementary at the same time. Masculine energy is hard on the outside but soft on the inside. Feminine energy is soft on the outside because of her intense power on the inside. We have countless examples from history of women controlling whole nations through their feminine power without lifting a finger themselves.

Without feminine energy, masculine energy can survive but it becomes overly critical and burdened without the nourishing life force from the feminine. Both energies truly depend on each other for survival and happiness. In Eastern cultures, it is believed that all things have aspects of the feminine and masculine. If I had to describe the two energies in the simplest terms possible, I would say that the masculine is structure, while the feminine is flow.

Feminine energy is the more luxurious energy. It requires nourishment, rest, feeling safe, and filling up with self care. Of course, the feminine energy in men needs these things too. Masculine energy can survive on no sleep, no food, and still go out hunting for three days. This was essential for the survival of our planet, can you see that? Women can "survive" and "hustle" in this way for a short period of time using their masculine energy. If they get stuck in their masculine energy for longer periods of time, the physical and emotional consequences are dire as their inner state and hormones are thrown off.

A woman who stays in her masculine energy for long periods of time signals to her primitive nervous system that "there is a crisis and there appears to be a shortage of men, stop all healing systems, all hands needed on deck." This is a red alarm, crisis situation for our delicate female hormones. We have not evolved to have this level of masculine energy running through our bodies. Doing masculine tasks actually disbalances our hormones. We simply don't have as much testosterone as men do. That is a scientific fact.

Men and women are designed to be able to access both the feminine and masculine within themselves. Ninety percent of women identify as primarily feminine essence which means they are attracted to masculine essence in their sexual partners. Ninety percent of men identify as primarily masculine essence which means they are attracted to feminine essence in their sexual partners. Most people flow back and forth between the two energies throughout the day but hold their dominant energy in romantic relationships to create polarity.

Masculine and Feminine energies attract each other like two opposite poles of a magnet. Just like two pluses repel each other, so do two people both in their masculine or alpha energy in relationships. This is clearly evident in same gender relationships, where one person is clearly more embodied in their masculine energy and the other in feminine energy. In heterosexual couples, we take these energies for granted.

We assume the woman is feminine and the man is masculine. However, the woman can be showing up in her masculine energy and therefore butting heads with her masculine husband.

We need to not only learn to balance these energies within us but also learn to use them consciously in relationships to create polarity. As you will learn in the next chapter, a happy whole person needs both masculine and feminine energies to live a happy and fulfilled life. When these energies are disbalanced or used in inharmonious ways, there can be severe consequences to our life, relationships, and happiness. Instead of looking at feminine and masculine energy as absolutes, start thinking of them as spectrums on a continuum. One question I want you to start asking yourself is: How much of feminine vs masculine energy am I running through my body right now?

My Story

I was born to Pakistani Immigrant parents in Chicago, IL in 1980. My parents were hard working, overly generous, loving but people-pleasing people. They lived life on a whim and often made crazy plans. (Like selling everything and moving out of the country with three kids only to move back in three months and start all over again.)

Dad was from a wealthy family who had come to the US in 1971 against his father's will. He had lived a sheltered, protected life where everything was done for him back home. The reality of being the first from his family to leave the country with no financial support from his father hit him hard. He worked hard and spent all his money on helping his siblings and friends come to the US. Not receiving much appreciation and seeing everyone else become more successful than him sent him into a deep depression and anxiety by the time I was a kid.

He married Sheena in early 1980 while on a trip back home visiting his family. Mom, or Sheena, as everyone lovely referred to her in her family, was from a lower middle class family. Her father was hit by a car and became unable to provide for his large family when Sheena was a teenager. Her oldest brother suddenly had to provide not only for his own wife and three kids, but also all nine of his family members.

In her culture, women are mostly provided for by men and rarely work outside the home. Things got tight and my mother got a job at a bank at age 16 to help make ends meet. Her childhood was cut short as she was placed in the masculine provider role for her family. This put her in her masculine energy. Sheena later confided in me that she was in love with a boy in her village but knew she wouldn't be able to help her family if she married him. She married my father at 19. He was from a wealthy family and lived in the US. She decided this union would help her family and agreed to the arranged marriage.

By the time her immigration was approved, she was already eight months pregnant with me. She landed in Chicago in October 1980 and I was born the following month. Although my dad very much wanted to provide for us, his inconsistent money habits put Sheena further into her masculine energy. I think she had lost her femininity because of her situation back home. Instead of inspiring Dad to get better with money, she often took things into her own hands by stepping into her masculine. She forgot that two masculine people can't have romance.

They were both generous, loving people who couldn't keep a penny to their name even if their lives depended on it. My mother went to work soon after my brother was born in 1984 and worked herself to the bone until her death at 49. In my early childhood, we were on and off of food stamps and other social services, and sometimes there was simply no food in the fridge.

Their crazy money habits and toxic generosity had dire consequences for me. By the time I was a teenager, I had been sexually molested three times, all by men my parents brought into our home. I called them The Strays. My parents had a big heart and they would take in anyone from their country who didn't have a place to live. I never heard my mother or father say no to someone in need. Even if that person was not a good person.

Speaking of home, I had over 30 addresses before I was old enough to drive, due to my parents changing their minds and uprooting our entire lives based on crazy ideas and sudden whims. I never felt safe or "at home" anywhere. There was a six-month homeless stretch when my father's best friend took the five of us into his tiny one-bedroom apartment. I was really embarrassed to impose on him in this way. He owed my dad for helping him come to the US.

Because of the lack of stability in my childhood, life was really inconsistent and rough. The good times were overshadowed by the trauma I faced in early childhood. During this time, I found a love of books. Books were and always will be my first love. I would max out the number of books you could check out on your library card. If we moved to an apartment where a library wasn't accessible, I would read and reread the books I had at home many times. Learning something new every time from the same beloved books.

Books were my happy place. They taught me of other places and possibilities for my life. I couldn't wait to become an adult and create my own life. I got my first job at 17. It was a retail job and I was so proud! At 18, I was promoted and moved into their corporate building. This was my first corporate job! At 19, I got an even better corporate job in a very wealthy neighborhood. My boss was so impressed that I worked full time while also going to school. I was quickly promoted to office manager in that company.

Suddenly, life was better. It felt like everything I touched turned to gold. I seemed to have the Midas touch with people. Everyone at work and school loved me. This version of my life seemed so different and way more exciting than my childhood. Even though I was very happy, I had a secret.

I suffered from massive panic attacks. They would happen anytime, anywhere. I would almost pass out sometimes and people would have to rush to my assistance. It was a whole scene! I had gotten good at hiding them for the most part and most people I knew didn't know about them. I was just so happy to have a life outside of home. I didn't want the panic attacks to hold me back in any way. I didn't know this at the time but because of my childhood trauma I was functioning overly in my masculine energy as a coping mechanism. More than a decade later, I was diagnosed with PTSD.

This inconsistent, chaotic upbringing has put me in massive fight or flight and overly reliant on my masculine energy. Remember that feminine energy requires feeling safe, which wasn't something I knew how to do at this point in my life.

Despite my less-than-ideal start to life, I finished high school early, graduated from Northwestern University, and had owned over 20 investment properties before my 27th birthday. I knew how to make money, that was for sure. I thought money was the only thing that could make me feel safe in my body. I did not realize that my nervous system didn't know how to metabolize safety. In my early and mid 20s I was making multiple six figures in my real estate business and going to school full time! I loved to learn and I loved to make money.

From my parents I learned that you can make money, but it wouldn't stay for long. No matter how much money they earned, they always seemed to give it away. So, this concept of having money, investing it, and then living off of it was something my brain couldn't even conceive.

Mother Wounds and Conditioning

Everything changed when I turned 16. My mother suddenly acknowledged my existence. Before this point, she was busy working, surviving, and trying to save her own family back home. My parents were hard working people with a whole host of their own human issues, limiting beliefs, and problems that I will never understand because I'm not them and have no idea what it's like to be an immigrant. They did the best they could from the level of consciousness and understanding they had.

Before 16, I was so lost in my own story and survival, I never realized their humanness. When Sheena suddenly woke up to my existence, I was awakened to how brilliant and amazing my mother was. Being the tough little 4'11 inches of a firecracker that she was, she found a way to continue her education in the US, hustle and literally support more than 10 families back home in addition to her own.

Sheena was literally a badass!! She worked 12 hour days most days that I knew her. Sometimes taking double shifts to support not only us but also her entire family back home. I never saw her sleep more than 3-4 hours a night. She never had the luxury of ever being sick or even getting a headache.

"*Getting sick requires time, I have too many mouths to feed,*" she would say. It was like she was numb to the fact that she even had a body or God forbid any other human needs. She paid for her growing extended family's daily expenses, education, marriages, babies, their children's schooling, bought them houses and cars, paid for health expenses, and countless desires until cancer took her in 2010. The second generation in her extended family didn't even get proper jobs because they knew Sheena would continue supporting them!

My mother's generosity turned into massive enabling at some point in the journey. She was addicted to giving. I think it was the only thing that gave her any personal significance. She became a social worker even in her community in Chicago, winning an award from the Major for all her work in community projects. Sheena impacted so many people over her short life, that her funeral caused major traffic jams forcing Chicago streets to be closed. People assumed some government official or celebrity had passed away.

I had a close relationship with Sheena from 1996 to 2010. I felt she was helping others at her own expense and I wanted her to take care of herself first and give from her overflow not from her depletion. I tried to knock some sense into her every now and then. She was never truly available for that conversation. In fact, she would often get upset with me so I would drop the topic.

When Sheena would run out of money, she would convince me to send money to her relatives. I had bought my cousin a plot and paid for the construction of her new home, while running her entire household and paying for her three kids' education before my 21st birthday. Did it feel good? I'm not sure. I have mixed feelings about the whole experience. I didn't love the part where we had to sacrifice our own needs and well-being in the name of charity. I could have put that money towards my own safety and security, or taken out less education loans. I also don't like the fact that my needs were once again put on the back burner in the name of helping others.

In my opinion, giving and charity should feel good, not ridden with guilt and obligation. The truth is, no one ever came to ask how my son and I were doing. In fact, these same people pointed a lot of fingers and spread rumors about me when I was going through my divorce. The only time they called was when they needed money. Did they even know that I was being molested in my own home while my parents were out working for them? I learned that I had to secure my own future first. Otherwise, my kids would be doomed to repeat the past.

This was the first layer of my personal savage awakening. I was starting to realize that Sheena's addictions to over-giving and people-pleasing directly conflicted with my desire to have money and finally feel safe in the world. It was really hard for me to stand up to my mom and tell her no on numerous occasions. It always seemed like her family had "good reasons" to need the money, but I was beginning to question if they were my problem.

Inner work happens in layers. You will find that deeply ingrained womb wounds or childhood conditioning often needs to be released in many different layers. It can be quite frustrating sometimes when something you have already overcome comes back again in new ways to be looked at again. I noticed that for me, it was setting boundaries that has taken the deepest layers of inner work. Just when I think I am an expert at setting boundaries, a new layer would show up, ready to be healed again.

I used to think that women who naturally had confidence and self love to set boundaries were born with it. They were the lucky bitches who had inherited how to do life right. I felt cursed with these behaviors I couldn't shed. Right when life was looking like it was in my control, I had to deal with all of these people with their hands in my pocket. Saying no to Sheena was so painful and hard especially when I wanted her love and attention so badly. But I also didn't want to end up like her.

Today, I enjoy giving generously from my overflow only to the people and places that feel good to my soul. I never allow anyone to guilt or shame me into giving. I see all people as fully capable of figuring it out for themselves. Don't be afraid to "close the door with love." "*That doesn't work for me*" is my favorite, simple, boundary setting statement. Remember this: Your family and friends will figure it out like you figured it out. Give only where it feels 100% good and only after you are safe and secure yourself. Otherwise they will never let you amass any sort of wealth!

Sidenote: I love to give generously to people who are "moving their hands and feet" and trying to make something of themselves. For example, I love overtipping but never give to panhandlers.

It seemed to me that Sheena was addicted to being the savior even at the expense of her own well-being. She told me once that she was known as the ugly sister in her family and the only value she brought to the family was her providing. Sheena's behavior was what can be referred to as a womb wound or generational curse. This means I was also infected with her trauma in utero. And then unknowingly conditioned and trained by Sheena to take over her trauma-led over-giving ways in my childhood on top of that.

We now have scientific evidence that proves that trauma is transferred in the womb. Most of our womb wounds come from the mother line. Mother line wounds are harder to break (not impossible, just more deeply ingrained.) We do inherit trauma through the sperm but it's not as deeply baked in. Since both my parents had the similar toxic giving behavior and money story, I got both the womb wounds and the conditioning.

Womb wounds are when trauma is passed down in the womb. DNA is a collection of data-sets of instructions telling your mind, body, and energy how to be and what to become. Conditioning is how you are taught to be and do life after you are born. Parental influence, extended family, culture, relationships, teachers, friends, society all contribute to our conditioning. You can learn a lot of your own conditioning and mindsets by observing your parents, grandparents, relatives, and earliest caregivers. Womb wounds are a level after DNA and a level before childhood conditioning. They are the epigenetics that take place in the womb.

Not all of it is bad of course. Just like you love some of the DNA traits you inherit and others not so much. Conditioning is also the same. I definitely got my entrepreneurial spirit and resourcefulness from my mother. And kindness and generosity from both my parents, which I choose to channel in less destructive ways than they did.

What's important here is the self-awareness to know what's theirs and what's ours. If you live life on autopilot, you end up living your entire life on someone else's conditioning. You never even realize your own soul blueprint, which is the thing God created you to be and do.

From Sheena, I also learned so much about womanhood and the silent suffering that often occupies being a daughter, sister, wife, mother, and the countless other roles a woman plays in her society. From my father I learned that men need to feel like the head of the household to be healthy. My mother often emasculated him and his contributions were not much celebrated or acknowledged by anyone. The sad truth is that my father's anxiety and depression actually healed after my mother passed away.

I also realize now that it was wrong of me to try to stop my mother from doing what she pleased with her hard-earned money. I'm happy she got to live her life exactly like she wanted it. Even if others didn't agree. That is an important lesson in boundaries for all of us. We may not always agree with everyone's decisions, but it's not our place to judge, object, or intervene.

As my mother got older and more and more burned out, I believe she started awakening to the truth. She didn't stop sending money back home, but she stopped pressuring me as much. Mainly because she started to realize that her family didn't really care about her or her kids. Also, because I set some strong energetic boundaries on what I was willing to do and not do with my money. More on energetic boundaries later.

We started to form an unspoken understanding that I would not end up like her. Even though her human part sometimes gave me a hard time when I said no to her requests to send her family more money. Or invest in her or dad's crazy spur of the money schemes. Her favorite thing to say to me was, "*I don't have to worry about you because you are too selfish.*" Strangely enough, it was Sheena who taught me the most savage of truths that I believe every woman should know. Some of which we will discuss in this book. Everything she didn't give herself permission to do or be, she wanted me to do and be.

Most of what Sheena said, I didn't take very seriously. Not because it wasn't great advice. But because my mother's health and life was such a hot mess, I didn't see her as someone worth taking advice from. This taught me a very important lesson: If you want people to take your advice, embody what you are teaching. The only other option is to be such a rock bottom hot mess, that they immediately choose to do everything opposite of you.

I choose to embody myself with everything I want to teach my children. Instead of telling them, I show them! Honestly, I didn't actually "get" Sheena until she passed away. Then it all suddenly sunk in. Her consciousness downloaded and merged within mine. Sheena was only a conditioned victim of her circumstances and like most people she never had the luxury of doing inner work.

This is why I call inner work a luxury. It really is a privilege. Not everyone has time, a safe space, and resources to invest into their personal growth. Most people are living on automated survival.

Sheena passed away in March of 2010. I created my YouTube channel in January 2011 as a part of my grieving process. I had this strong, undeniable desire to connect with women. God had plans for me bigger than I was ready to understand at that point. Initially the channel helped me grieve my own pain, then start deep healing inner work, and then helping others from my overflow. I too wanted to help people like Sheena, but only from my overflow. Never at mine or my family's expense.

As my channel grew and I had more and more access to women from all walks of life, stages, and statuses, it suddenly became clear to me. My mother's journey wasn't just her story. We were all beholden to societal roles in unconscious ways. Sheena was like a female computer program, coded through generations of women suffering and sacrificing their own happiness and joy for others.

She became almost this symbol of women everywhere. Suffering in silence. Representing the collective struggles of women of all cultures. Her potential and genius was cut short because of her neglecting her own health. In the few years before her cancer diagnosis, Sheena was earning $350,000 a year in her real estate business. Not bad for someone who had the most basic education from a third world country and barely spoke English!

During this time she received many signs that she needed serious medical care but she refused to take the time to go to the doctor. Sheena was the golden goose that slaughtered herself. Despite working herself literally to death, she had nothing to show for it. Her charity was never much appreciated or accounted for. Even in her direst need she was sending all her money back home. We found the bank wire receipts after her death.

I am not Sheena. I am her evolution. The next gen technological advancement to her DNA. I'm here to break the generational curse of scarcity, self-sacrifice, and suffering. I owe my ancestors as much. This is how I see it… every single woman before me was "sacrificing" her own happiness and joy to help someone else. But that someone else also did the same, and so on and so forth. This sounds like a really hellish pyramid scheme where NO ONE actually benefits.

Everyone is miserable. WTF. No thank you. I refuse to co-sign that. I opt out. Instead, I get to be the one that actually cashes in my inheritance. "*It is my God-given right to live life on my own terms.*"

I am that powerful single point in the blood line that breaks out of suffering and scarcity, changing my family's morphogenetic field. Rewriting the code for my children and their children. Sheena's legacy deserves a daughter that manifested and lived out her every single desire!

Through my embodiment and modeling, my daughter will know her worth and value. She will learn to fully receive life and its many blessings and give only from her overflow… if and when she feels like it.

I am the legacy line breaker. I am the Golden Sheep. I owe it to my ancestors and descendants to live my best life, and so do you!

The day Sheena passed, only days before her 50th Birthday, I was eight months pregnant with my second son. Placed on bed rest because of a complicated pregnancy. In the deepest grief of my life. Sheena's family, the ones she supported her entire life, called me. I thought it was a call acknowledging our collective immense loss. Instead, they had called to confirm I would continue sending them money now that my mother couldn't.

It wasn't a call of condolences. It was a call securing their own future by the next generation of dummies. I had one hand on my pregnant belly and the other held the phone to my ear. At this time in my life, I was a stay at home mom, pregnant with my second child, on bed rest, grieving my mom. And there they were, expecting a lifetime of financial support from me.

I would either have to convince my husband that I came as a package with at least 25 other grown, fully capable people to support. Or option two, become Sheena, put my kids in childcare, and get a job to support them. Continuing the womb wounds and conditioning she had passed on to me.

It took me a split second to make the decision. I hung up the call and had my number changed.

Activate Lady Luck by Choosing Yourself

I choose myself. And because I choose myself, I don't have to wait 16 years to have a relationship with my kids. My kids feel safe in their home because their parents are emotionally and physically available to create a safe, sacred, home environment. My children get to be the priority in their home and life.

It has now been 13 years since my mom's passing and that last phone conversation with her relatives. And guess what? They are all living. Some started businesses, others finally got jobs, and some found other relatives to support them. Meanwhile, I got to raise my kids and create a beautiful life for myself and my family in financial peace. Problem solved. No sacrifice needed.

I didn't have to continue the savior legacy coming down my mother line. I saw them as more resourceful and capable than Sheena did and they lived up to it. I used my "Be a Bitch Once" technique here which I can't wait to share with you in a future chapter. I hope this technique helps you as much as it has in my life!

In the famous words of Mother Teresa, "*If you want to save the world, go home and love your family.*"

I am home.

There is no family without the feminine.

Women are the life force of society.

Nothing works when we are depleted, empty, and tired. Without us, our men become lost and our children become anxious. It's high time we reset society to honor the truth of the Divine Feminine's rightful position in the heart and soul of the planet.

Remember: There is no qualification or certification for parenting. Your parents are average people with their own stuff to deal with. Their stuff becomes your stuff unless you are self-aware enough to break the patterns. Going against our family conditioning is not easy but it's necessary if you want to live a better life than they did. Expecting them to have stellar parenting skills simply because they are your parents is delusional. Start seeing them as human with their own stuff to deal with and you will immediately overcome half your battles and stories.

Lesson: Examine your womb wounds and conditioning unless you are happy to become a replica of your ancestry and closest family and friends.

Journal Prompts:

What are the womb wounds and conditioning I inherited from my mother? What conditioning did I receive from my father? What did I learn from other important caregivers or family members?

What did I learn from them about success, money, womanhood?

How are these things still impacting me now in positive or negative ways?

CHAPTER *Three*

BABES, BARBIES, AND LUCKY BITCHES

Some women are born knowing their place in the world, feeling comfortable in their own skin, and confident in navigating the world and setting boundaries. It's hitting the genetic and conditioning lottery jackpot! When they enter the room, people immediately know not to mess with them without any conscious effort on their part. They have careers where their contributions are celebrated and well respected. They have love and respect in their relationships. Let's call them our special unicorn women.

I was not born that woman and I bet neither were you. I was born a people-pleaser and over-giver, and constant over-doer, infected in the womb with many generations of over-giving and people-pleasing in my lineage from both sides of the DNA line. Confused with my worth and place in the world, trying to become worthy through servitude. I was a girl with a big heart that often got stepped all over and taken advantage of. The one that loved and gave so much, but somehow it was never enough.

For most women, personal power, boundaries, a sense of self, and self-esteem are hard learned skill sets. For the special unicorn women born with unlimited confidence and self-esteem, the principles in this book come naturally. I have spent over four decades learning and embodying the principles I am about to share with you. I have also helped hundreds of thousands of women do the same through my free online content, over 60 digital courses, and in person events.

For the special unicorn women, these principles may seem harsh, mean, or even downright unloving. They do not understand the psychology and energetic makeup of the womb-infected people-pleasers and over-givers. Reading a book on boundaries doesn't suddenly undo generations of programming trapped in our DNA and cellular memory. **We must learn to "overcorrect" by being a savage or what most would call a "bitch" to land in the happy middle space of healthy relationships with self and others.**

Sure, you can skip the savage and simply move in tiny little steps towards setting boundaries and try very hard not to overgive. Many people spend an entire life trying to get over their natural tendencies and deeply rooted habits. I tried it the slow and "normal" way, but it didn't work. The truth is that it could never work because the people I was dealing with were savage. They were the kind of savage with bad intentions.

The evil savage. A dangerous mix. The predators who use, manipulate, and energetically rape people.

If you complain to friends and family members, you will soon get vanilla advice like, "state your boundaries," or "have a heart-to-heart talk with them." You know better. You can't sit these people down and reason with them. Conversations on boundaries end up with you being further manipulated and mind-fucked. Being direct, clear, and using power poses make you seem like an even bigger idiot for trying.

As you will learn in this book, savage requires savage. Power requires Power. What you hold in your hands is a manifesto of the savage knowledge that should have been rightfully yours at birth. It was denied, stripped away, deconditioned out of you, leaving you with a wounded sense of self and nothing in your toolbox that works with the type of people you encountered in your life journey. In fact, not being savage makes you a very attractive opportunity for those that like to prey on others.

All your good intentions, desires, plans, and goals will be useless if your emotions can be hijacked by manipulators or people simply being envious of you. You will notice the savage advice sprinkled all throughout this book. Without that awakening, there is no way I would be where I am today. My unusual success despite my upbringing has come with the integration of both my spiritual and human, embodying both masculine and feminine energies, at the intersection of divinity and savageness. There is no easy way to say this. You will have to shed the womb wounds and conditioning, and function with your full range to be a successful woman in today's world.

Here is what I want you to know: Predators are more animal than human. Because of this, we can never really "out predator" them. Just like you wouldn't need decades of therapy or forgiveness exercises if a wolf ate your chickens, because you have accepted wolves as predators, you need to see them for what they are. People waste way too much time trying to get an apology, validation, or closure from animals in human bodies. **READ: Predators don't have access to the consciousness you are hoping to awaken in them. They don't have the moral compass that you do.**

When loving, kind, sincere, honest, compassionate people like you follow savage principles, they ditch the deeply rooted people-pleasing, over-giving, doormat DNA while still retaining all their love and kindness. You won't suddenly become evil or mean because of your divine part. People who benefit from manipulating you may call you those names, but you will never become that.

Adding savage power to your loving embodiment makes you stronger and more loving in your embodiment. We need more kind hearted, loving people in positions of power. Being a source of inspiration, power, and abundance on this planet is not only your birthright but also all of ours to witness through your embodiment. **We need loving, kind-hearted people to be as equally, if not more, scary and dangerous to predators as they are to us and our children.**

I'm sure I have been called every name in the book. It's a small price to pay for the widely successful life I have created. The energy that was freed up by letting go of parasites and leeches has been since used to create legacy love, unlimited energy, health, happy thriving relationships, and a God-led eight-figure business I am so damn proud of. Meanwhile restoring my faith in humanity and divinity.

Mina's Stages of Consciousness

As we have been learning, our DNA, womb wounds, and childhood conditioning all shape who we become. All this shapes our identity and how we show up in this world. I have developed a framework and tool to help myself and my students see where they are in their inner work journey and what next steps will help them most.

Basic Babe™

Self-Aware Barbie™

Million Dollar Babe™

High End Divinity™

These stages are meant to be used as a guide to help you select the best inner work tools and techniques for yourself. They are not meant to be weaponized against yourself or others. Please be kind and respectful of everyone's journey. Especially your own. I find most people to be a mixture of these 4 levels. It's best to think of these stages not as an on/off switch, but instead as a dimmer switch. A fluid continuum of stages and levels that we ebb and flow through.

Most people have one dominant stage where they spend the most time. Others have one stage and then fall into a lower stage when triggered. Which one is your dominant stage most of the time? And also, which stage is activated when you are triggered?

It may also be helpful to see each stage as split into three parts. With the third stage merging with the level above it. These stages can exist in percentages within the same person. For example, you could be 50% Basic Babe and 50% Self-Aware Barbie.

Basic Babe

A Basic Babe is in the wounded inner child stage. In this stage, one sees themselves as powerless and as victims to people, places, and circumstances. Entitlement can also be a huge issue in this stage. They can be very childish in their mental processing and reasoning especially when triggered.

People in this stage are dependent on others to get their basic physical and emotional needs met. From their point of view, someone else is held responsible for their survival and wellbeing. That someone could be parents, siblings, romantic partners, friends or the government.

The Basic Babe is the forever damsel in distress and massive victim-hood. Everything is happening to the Basic Babe. She has no sense of responsibility and has given away her personal power to people, places, and circumstances. She is addicted to drama, complaining, and has low self-worth. She is often not receptive to love due to constricted heart center and low self-worth. Often addicted to drama, food, or gossip. Hoping to find a man to take care of her so she can go from mommy and daddy to someone else providing. A lot of her energy is used up in finding and keeping a man or drama with friends.

You are a Basic Babe, if you…

- Have trouble creating plans, structures, goals, and sticking to them.
- Have trouble making money and mostly rely on other people for manifesting things or money in your life.
- You are easily triggered and often lose control of your senses and emotions when in a triggered state.
- Feel like everyone is out to get you. It's always someone else's fault why you are not happy and successful in life.
- It always feels like you need someone else's permission before making even the simplest decisions in your life.
- Feel very dependent on others to get your basic emotional, physical, and financial needs met.
- Lack a sense of direction and purpose in your life.

If you relate to this, start your inner work immediately. I recommend finding a great therapist either in your area or online. You will need to do some inner child work and heal your mother and father wounds before advancing to the next stage. This will help activate your personal power and healthy masculine energy in your life. You can find additional resources in the resources section of this book.

Self-Aware Barbie

Self-Aware Barbie is the wounded masculine/feminine stage. This stage is activated when a woman's fight/flight response is turned on through life trauma or conditioning, putting the woman in her wounded masculine. This doesn't have to be something big like in my case. It could be as simple as growing up with a super masculine mother in a masculine society where achievements and structure are celebrated more than intuition and play. The Self-Aware Barbie takes personal responsibility for her triggers. In fact, she may overly blame herself even when it's not her fault! She catches her triggers and is actively working to rewire her neural pathways. She is taking back her personal power via hard work and determination. She is a go-getter, please-pleaser and overgiver. Usually has an over-developed masculine side. Heart center is beginning to open as she becomes more receptive, especially in stage three. SABs are great at creating structures and disciplines for themselves and others.

An important thing to consider about SABs is that they activate the "predator" response in even generally good people. The truth is that most people are somewhere in the middle of the human vs divine spectrum. They are generally good but may choose to act questionably when the opportunity presents itself. Remember the saying, "Give them a finger and they will take a hand?" When the Self-Aware Barbie shows up knowing it all, doing it all, and giving it all, it awakens entitlement and even predatory behavior in others. I personally seem to have a PhD in awakening the "I am entitled to your time and energy" response from all kinds of people. I have seen countless fully grown, capable people act like they own me. This has been a continued journey of inner work on my part. If you deal with this, the tips in the following chapters will help you free yourself from this energy.

Self-Aware Barbie Phases

Phase one SAB is part Basic Babe and part SAB. She can get a job, make money, be resourceful, and independent when needed. However, she has a high addiction to drama and victimhood. She won't let any opportunity go for a good fight, argument, or text message battle. She sees herself being the victim even though the whole thing is often facilitated by her. She will often ask really disempowering and even childish questions. In this stage, our SAB has less structure and more chaos.

She is beginning to use her masculine energy to build something for herself. However, her feminine energy is still wounded and coming through in a disempowered, childish way. Going back to our fight or flight example, she is more fight than flight. Her drama extends from getting into comment wars on social media, group messaging battles with family and friends, and issues with co-workers and clients that limit her riches drastically!!

If there was a message I could give to the phase one SAB, it would be: Girl, stop it! You are stunting your growth and leaving money on the table. Use the techniques I shared in this book to give drama the boot once and for all! You are meant for riches and a divinely luxurious lifestyle. Drama has no room in your world, well, okay maybe in your bold outfit, but that's about it! It will always look like someone else is starting it since you have managed to collect drama addicted people around you. You will have to outgrew it fast and evolve out of it even if it means losing some friendships.

Phase two SAB is the information spitter. In this phase, the SAB is keeping herself busy and away from drama. She busies herself with her education and learning new things. Which is amazing and we are so proud of her! She gets obsessed with topics and literally gets a PHD in every topic she finds interesting. She is the queen at creating structures but not very good at getting into flow. The issue? She isn't embodying all of it yet but instead leaking energy by giving others unsolicited advice and coaching for free with her newfound information. Most of the people she preaches to, unfortunately, are not interested in learning something from a disembodied teacher. And because of this she often feels very unseen, unheard, and misunderstood.

In this stage, she is using mostly her masculine energy at the expense of her femininity. And for the record, this has nothing to do with how someone looks. You can be the most girly girl in your makeup and attire, and spend your entire day in your masculine energy.

Message for SAB phase two: God gave you this information for YOU. It's yours to keep, enjoy, and embody. This is not the time to share unless someone explicitly asks and better yet, exchanges money with you. Remember that complaining and venting are not invitations for advice. Most people don't actually want to change and will actually become resentful if you try to solve the problems they are addicted to. Use what you are learning for your own benefit. Once you fully embody it, the right people will be coming to you begging for your secrets.

This happened to me when I was diagnosed with rheumatoid arthritis in 2012. I refused medication and threw myself in 8 hours of daily study of nutrition and other lifestyle changes. I was reading, watching YouTube, and listening to interviews, documentaries, and podcasts for 8 hours a day, for 7 years straight! Pretty soon I had not only healed my autoimmune disease but knew more than the average doctor in the United States about nutrition. Only 25% of US medical schools teach nutrition and it's only one class, so as you can imagine, even doctors were impressed with the information I now had.

In the beginning of my journey, especially as I started seeing fast results, I started warning everyone about the dangers of their dietary choices and lifestyle habits. As you can imagine, no one wanted to hear it! I was still dealing with joint pain, hair loss, skin rashes, and fatigue, why would anyone listen to me! The changes that had started were only on the inside. No one could see the results yet. Keep in mind that not everyone wants a solution.

Years later when my disease was healed and long forgotten from my mind, I had a full head of hair, glowing skin, and had lost a ton of weight, everyone wanted to find out my secrets! In fact, people were willing to pay me money for it. Same information, different levels of embodiment. Lesson learned! Now I embody first and let them pay me for the information if they want it. No spitting out of information or unsolicited coaching!

Another issue with this stage is the inability to surrender and let go of control. This can make relationships really difficult. Even as a coach working with SAB phase two can present some challenges. They come in as a client and often want to rearrange my business or coach me, LOL. At my in-person events, stage two SAB often keeps running out of the room asking hotel staff for this or that. No one asked them to be the help, but they struggle being a guest! Having strong boundaries really helps when dealing with SABs in phase two.

Phase three SAB: This stage is my absolute favorite level to work with! In this stage, our SAB has had some encounters of flow and surrender. She has not quite mastered full energy fluidity like the Million Dollar Babe but the desire has been awakened for more! In this stage, the SAB doesn't need more information, she needs activations and transmissions from an embodied mentor. She needs examples and inspirations. Sort of like a four minute mile to fully break through her limiting beliefs around femininity, ease, and flow. In fact, in this stage, giving them too much information may trigger them back to stage two.

Our SAB is finally starting to activate her feminine energy in addition to her already cultivated masculine side. She isn't intentional or fully conscious of this yet, but it's definitely a step in the right direction! This stage overlaps with the Million Dollar Babe stage one. If you spend more time in your SAB than your MDB then you are phase three SAB. If you spent more time in your MDB, than your SAB, then you are stage one MDB.

This is the stage I spent my life in from ages 16-33 and the reason I manifested my autoimmune disease. It's like an eternal fight or flight switch turns on and you realize you can't really depend on others around you. Despite massive trauma in my childhood, I didn't have the luxury of becoming a Basic Babe. I didn't trust others to support me in any way. The only option then was to do it all yourself and trust no one. As a feminine essence woman, this became a direct conflict to how I wanted to live and be treated in relationships.

Of course, there is nothing wrong with being resourceful and independent. I still value these traits in myself and others. The issue is that this "I gotta do it all myself and can't trust anyone" attitude is coming from a fight or flight place. About 80% of the women who find my work online are in the Self-Aware Barbie phase three. After serving tens of thousands of women in this stage through my courses and group coaching programs, I have a deep-seated knowledge and understanding of the mindsets and behaviors stemming from this consciousness.

Self-Aware Barbies are highly self-motivated and high achieving women. I absolutely adore their strong work ethics and success drive. They cross their Ts and dot their Is. They are highly educated and strive to become as humanly successful as they can. All of these are amazing things that I also did. The issue is that since they are doing this from an injured intuition and survival place, they lean on their masculine side at the expense of their feminine side, often burning out and making things way more complicated than needed.

As women when we are in fight or flight, we immediately go into our masculine energy. To make matters more complicated, western society in recent decades has disproportionately started favoring masculine energy traits over feminine energy. In order to create anything beautiful and pleasurable, we need both the masculine and feminine polarities. Not just one.

A baby requires both the egg and the sperm. Money requires both energies, attracting it and keeping it. Business requires both as well, the art form and the structure holding and selling the art form. Life gave us both energies for a reason. Attraction definitely requires polarity. This is true in every romantic relationship, not only heterosexual relationships. All relationships will have one person primarily holding the masculine energy and the other holding the feminine.

Unfortunately, our schools and corporations reward mostly masculine traits such as setting goals, keeping time/space, thinking logically/rationally, creating structures, competing, being accountable, and keeping score. This makes it even easier for Self-Aware Barbies to get stuck in this stage on masculine auto-pilot. Feminine traits such as timelessness, intuition, play, rest, feelings, flow, collaboration, creativity, and enjoying the journey are often seen as lazy or weak. These are the very qualities that add magic to our lives. Feminine traits make life worth experiencing for both men and women.

Masculine energy was a fail-safe mechanism in women. We were never designed to be stuck in this mode for long periods of time. We simply don't have the same testosterone as men to be able to run masculine energy in the ways currently expected of us in society. Women who are living mostly in their masculine energy and never have a break to recharge and rest through the feminine end up with all kinds of relationship and health issues. Their general satisfaction and happiness in life also suffers. Which in turn affects their families' well-being.

Lack of romance in relationships, loss of libido, burnout, adrenal fatigue, autoimmune issues, and other deadly diseases are just some of the side-effects of women overusing their masculine energy. I absolutely adore nature for giving us the Self-Aware Barbie stage as an option and beautiful range. When used correctly, this stage is what gives us our resourcefulness, ability to set goals, and see them through. This stage saved my life at a time when I needed it most in my teens and all of my 20s but it also burned me out and caused numerous health and relationship issues.

When I married my husband in 2008, he retired me from my business. I had the perfect chance to rest, rejuvenate, and truly feel safe for the first time in my life. However, because I only knew how to be a Self-Aware Barbie, my nervous system was very restless and unable to adapt to my new pace of life for a long while. I only knew how to be in my masculine energy most of the time. I didn't really know how to enjoy my femininity. Without my business to keep my masculine energy occupied, I started showing up in masculine ways in my marriage. And the romance went out the door pretty quickly at that point because two alphas can't create polarity!

Being in my masculine most of the time also caused a lot of health and other issues. Integrating and evolving out of the SAB stage was honestly the best thing that happened to me! Living primarily in your feminine energy and using your masculine energy in conscious, intentional ways instead of fight or flight is so nourishing!! It makes life seem magical and orgasmic!

Integrating my femininity back into my life made me so much more powerful as a woman. I got healthier, my fibroids, adrenal fatigue, hair loss, skin rashes, and not to mention rheumatoid arthritis, all went away. I honestly credit the Million Dollar Babe stage for my romantic, healthy marriage, great health and energy, happy home, spirituality and all my financial and life success! This is what I help my clients and students do. Integrate the SAB from a healthy place and then move on to the Million Dollar Babe stage.

You are a Self-Aware Barbie, if you...

- Are highly self-motivated and high achieving in your studies and career.
- Need to control everything and need things to be perfect to feel good.
- Feel like no one else can do it like you and therefore often refuse support.

- Can juggle many tasks and to do lists and are always looking to add more things to your plate.
- Have trouble relaxing and resting, there is always so much more to do.
- Often get taken advantage of in relationships because of your over giving and people-pleasing nature.
- Typically outperform the men in your life in basically every area of life.
- Have trouble in romantic relationships because men are intimidated by you.
- Consider yourself and/or are considered by others an Alpha female.
- Look powerful on the outside but often feel weak and scared on the inside.
- Have trouble accessing your emotions and often feel numb to pleasure.

If this is you, you need feminine energy inner work yesterday!! Self-Aware Barbies make the ideal clients and students for my body of work. Through reclaiming your feminine power, nervous system reprogramming, and activating flow states, you become a healed whole being and start to function at full capacity. Imagine learning that one of your hands was tied behind your back all along. You accomplished all that you did with just one arm!! As amazing and admirable as that is, it's also exhausting. I have been there and I know what that burn out feels like. Imagine what you could do and be if all of you were in sync and harmonious. This is what living in alignment truly means.

The reason these two lower stages are becoming more and more common in society right now is because of the absence of maternal presence in the first three years of life. According to Psychoanalyst, Author, and Parent Coach Erica Komisar, there should be as little as possible separation between the mother and baby in the first three years. Babies learn to manage their emotions and place in the world through attunement with their mother in these formative years. The mom not only needs to be physically but also emotionally present for the child to develop in a healthy way mentally and physically. Licensed professional counselor, Kelly McDaniel refers to the absence of loving, safe, maternal presence in these early years as mother hunger, in her book, Mother Hunger.

Modern day parents have been sold the lie of babies needing socialization in daycares and many who are able to stay home decide not to. The child, having been robbed of the attunement with the mother, develops coping mechanisms to deal with life. The Basic Babe becomes hungry for attention and affection, which will resort to creating drama or problems to get attention from anyone, not realizing she internally deeply craves mother 's presence. This may start early on as a toddler throwing tantrums and a child in school unable to focus and learn. The Self-Aware Barbie chooses her achievements, over-giving, over-doing, people-pleasing as her coping mechanism hoping to win the love that was her God-given birthright all along.

This is not to blame mothers but allows parents to make the first three years the most important time for their children's entire life. Finding this research led to a double grieving process in my life. I first had to grieve the loss of not having my mother present and available when I was born, resulting in over 40 years of inner work. I know my mother wanted to be there but my parents needed both incomes and life was stressful for them as immigrants. Secondly, I had to grieve my first son's lack of maternal presence. When Armaan was born, I was in the middle of a very stressful divorce, a student at Northwestern University, and running a real estate business. He rarely had time with me. Contrary to popular belief, quality time is not the same as quantity of time. He needed me there all the time.

Luckily, both my son and I had the luxury of doing inner work because we knew this as an option and solution to not having the essential pair bonding time in the first three years of his life. It makes me sad to think that most people spend their entire life suffering and have no idea inner work was even an option.

I will now share with you the two healed stages of consciousness from my work. Remembering that healed doesn't mean your inner work has ended, inner work happens in layers and there is always room for improvement.

Million Dollar Babe

The Million Dollar Babe is the stage of Feminine/Masculine healing and integration. In this stage, surrender is a natural way of being because we trust in love and feel safe in our body and in the world. The Million Dollar Babe lives in divine flow, utilizing the beautiful structures she has created in her life. Because she is intuitive and fully receptive to her spirit and angel guides, this manifesting babe never feels or works alone. She is fully balanced and fluid in her masculine/feminine energies. This manifesting queen is vulnerable, sensual, and fully embodied in her delicious worthiness. Her heart is fully open and rests in warmth, faith, and love. This is the "lucky bitch" stage where everyone assumes our MDB is just born lucky, not realizing this is a learned and embodied stage and they too can activate it.

In this fully integrated frequency, the left and right sides of the brain are perfectly in sync and working together, giving you what may seem like superhuman abilities. This means you are experiencing moments of what is known as the zone or flow. Since you are perfectly balanced in your feminine and masculine energies, you can switch and sway between the two very easily. This is how we would naturally be if the mother wound hadn't occurred in our early formative years. However, me and my clients and students have had to reparent ourselves to learn this essential way of living and being.

You are a Million Dollar Babe, if you…

- Are able to flow fluidly between your masculine and feminine energies.
- Know how and when to create polarity with your romantic partner.
- Trust that the world is good and the Universe is always working in your favor.

- Have no trouble manifesting your desires and normalizing them once they arrive.
- You are able to create money with ease and flow and exponentially grow your wealth through investing.
- Have a great relationship with your intuition and can make decisions easily.
- Live in your overflow and are able to feel and amplify pleasure in every area of your life.
- Are able to stay in your zone of genius and access flow states, making everything you touch turn to gold.
- Everyone around you thinks you were born lucky because you make everything look effortless and easy.
- Win in relationships because of your strong sense of self and energetic boundaries.
- Don't get triggered very often and know exactly how to process your emotions if you do without having to throw them out on anyone else.

If you identify with this stage, appreciate and enjoy everything you have created while still learning and expanding into more. Healed and whole people like you are essential role models for society. You are contributing to the morphogenetic field for all others around you. You may have your moments of doubt when you surround yourself with people who are suffering, but never feel guilty for what you have and who you are. Your unapologetic light and radiance are necessary ingredients for the healing of all women on this planet, especially at this time. You are the four-minute mile society needs right now, always remember that.

High End Divinity

This is the stage of oneness in all things. In this stage, we move from manifesting it to becoming it. High End Divinity is my word for high priestess. In this stage you are more activated in your consciousness and metaphysical self than in your human animal self. In simple terms, you're able to turn off the amygdala and keep that fight or flight response almost always turned off, increasing your presence in the now. This doesn't mean you spiritually bypass your human experience, but it does mean you are more aware of and connected with the spiritual aspects of your being. You are the observer versus the reactor to most things in life. Which eliminates very high or low emotional waves.

You are a High-End Divinity, if you…

- Have manifested everything you have desired and more for yourself and now want to help others through your overflow.
- Rarely ever get triggered and actually end up helping the people triggering you.
- Give more than you take from the world and the quantum field.
- Are aware of other timelines and lifetimes beyond just this one.
- Are able to jump and collapse timelines at the speed of light.

If you identify with this stage, you have the ability to self regulate and coach yourself back into alignment and are probably only using me as a peer group grid to collaborate and create with.

Journal Prompts:

Which of the four stages is my dominant stage at this point in my journey?

Which stage am I in when I am triggered?

What can I do to elevate myself into the next state? What parts of me would need to heal to move to the next stage?

CHAPTER *Four*

EVERYONE IS ADDICTED TO SUFFERING

When I was seven months pregnant with my daughter, I found myself awake and anxious at 3am in the morning. My husband and kids were sound asleep. The house was quiet, and there I was worrying about how we were going to pay for the kids' college. My oldest was nine at the time, close to a decade away from going to college. I should also mention that we had just hit our first million net worth that year.

We could obviously afford to pay for college, but there I was, laying there crippled with fear and anxiety about something that hadn't actually happened yet. I was mentally trying to solve a problem that didn't exist, which was a nasty habit of mine at the time. Turns out you can't really solve problems that actually haven't happened yet. What a waste of precious energy!

Up until this point in my journey, I would make up scenarios in my mind and then spend days, weeks, months worrying about them! Just writing this down on paper sounds completely insane! So, imagine my relief when I discovered we are designed by nature to do this! In fact, our ancestors survived because of their ability to project and worry about worst case scenarios and then take action.

I realized this was something I was going to need to work really hard at overcoming. Not only for my own peace of mind and general life satisfaction, but also because the predatory people in my life often used this tendency against me. Manipulators know exactly what to say to you to gain access to this primitive, human worry machine part of your brain. **Read this twice: If they can get you in your amygdala, the part of the brain responsible for fight or flight, you are easier to control, manipulate, humiliate, and whatever else they want to do with you!**

Gaining emotional mastery is the #1 thing you can do to make yourself less attractive to predators.

I noticed that when I would be having an exceptionally wonderful day, looking good, feeling good, certain friends and family members would say things to get me back into my fight or flight. I always like to give people the benefit of the doubt but when my husband and oldest son started to point this out, I became more aware of it. Then I caught them snickering after making me really worried and anxious! I knew at that point that I would never let anyone have that sort of power over me and my emotions! Makes me so sad to think that some people actually thrive out of making others worry!

The truth is, most of your problems are imaginary. Yes, your brain makes up imaginary problems and then terrorizes you with them. Studying anthropology and evolution both in university and as a personal obsession most of my adult life, I couldn't help but notice one common and loud tread in our evolutionary history: Life was freaking hard for our ancestors. The more I studied our hunter-gatherer ancestors, the more I realized how lucky we all have it. Yes, even the worst of the situations happening to us are a huge upgrade from our earliest ancestors. Food was scarce, terrains were harsh and cold, and they were often surrounded by predators and lost half of their offspring and other tribe members due to the most simple illnesses caused by lack of proper hygiene. They often went weeks and sometimes even months without eating!

As a result of this programming, we evolved a brain that was massively addicted to suffering. Our primitive brain developed in times of extreme hardships. It's not going to suddenly evolve out of millions of years of programming just because we traded jungles for cities. We still carry that primitive part of our brain with us to this day. Although life looks very different now with our modern housing, technology, food, and societal advances, our brain has not received the memo. Evolution takes time and hundreds or not thousands of generations to make even the simplest dent in our physical makeup. This is known as the evolution gap.

Advancement happened way faster than it takes human evolution to catch up. Your brain is still wired to perceive survival threats and worry about them constantly. Think of it this way, those who worried about the potential loss of food or life in those dangerous terrains, did something about it and survived. We are the descendants of the hunter-gatherers who worried and found problems to solve. And since life is really really good now compared to our early ancestors, your brain literally makes shit up, and then wastes precious energy trying to solve imaginary problems. Regardless of your current personal situation, the truth is that as a species, we are the safest, most prosperous we have ever been.

Evolution takes time. Consciousness does not. So, you can use your conscious awareness to evolve out of our collective pre-programmed addictions to suffering or you can continue being a slave to your brain. Just a small glimpse of how our ancient addictions to suffering show up in modern ways.

- Making life and tasks way more complicated than they need to be.
- Perceiving imaginary threats and then wasting time trying to problem solve them even though they haven't occurred yet.
- Keeping ourselves small for fear of success.
- Being afraid of change.
- Being afraid of standing out and "upsetting the other tribe members".

- Creating and prolonging drama so we can get our dose of addictions to suffering and feel like we are working hard to solve problems and therefore advancing.
- Choosing friends or a romantic partner makes our life overly complicated.

Your colleague in the cubicle next to you is turned into a potential security threat as your brain makes up stories of him stealing your work, your job, or just being better favored by your boss. Your mother-in-law takes the literal shape of a predator out to turn your husband against you. Food is no longer scarce or dangerous to obtain in the way it was for our hunter-gatherer ancestors but we have transferred our poverty mindset onto money and belongings. Notice how we worry and obsess over things that haven't even happened yet.

We have little history and experience with the kind of abundance we currently have available on this planet. Surviving prosperity with a brain addicted to suffering is the new human dilemma. We are one of the most prosperous and technologically advanced human beings to have walked this planet. We also seem to be the most lost, anxious, and depressed. The modern human still thinks and acts like hunter-gatherers in our everyday lives and doesn't even realize it. As modern day homo sapiens, we must use our self-awareness and consciousness to evolve our brain out of this addiction to suffering. This is where inner work comes in.

Predators, Who They are and What They Want from Us

Before, I continue with the techniques that helped me break the addictions to suffering not only for myself but also for tens of thousands of my students, let's discuss predators. All human beings are part human and part divine. Our humanness grounds us to this planet and is our connection to the animal kingdom and tied to our evolutionary history. Our divinity is the part that makes us a child of God. It's the part tied to our consciousness, creativity, oneness with all things, and gives us access to the metaphysical realms. Most humans fall somewhere in the middle of the human/divine spectrum. Then we have the outliers we may refer to as saints, monks, and other extraordinary people who are more divine than human. These amazing individuals clearly seem to have more access to the celestial realms than the rest of us.

Predators are the outliers in the other direction. They are more human, almost animal like in their makeup and consciousness. It is important for you to understand that they do not feel, think, or behave like you and me. This is why trying to reason with them or emotionally appeal to them in any way does not work. Their brain is wired differently than yours, they perceive the world very differently as well. I sat through hours of interviews of convicted predators, as part of a class assignment in university, simply fascinated how someone can look so "human" and be so "animal." They look like us but they think and behave like predatory animals.

One way this makes sense to me is how there are many different types of cats, lizards, and birds. All a little different in how they act and behave, although they all belong to the same larger "family". Predators are a slight split off from the human race. They look and act like us in many ways but are also vastly different. They have less access to their heart, the part tied to our intuition, kindness, love, generosity, and empathy, and more access to their animalistic instincts.

It is also important to note that there is a little "predator" or animal part in all of us. This is the part that gives us access to dark energy when needed. Our hunter ancestors needed this part to hunt animals for food and to defend themselves and their tribes. This is a necessary part of our physical makeup. As someone who has the tendency to over give, people-please, and other overdoing behaviors, you have to look out not only for evil predators, but also everyone else's natural predatory tendencies. **Read this twice: People like us can activate the predator instincts even in normal, generally good people.**

Sheena's family were not evil predators. In fact, they were loving, kind people who took advantage of her generosity because the opportunity presented itself. Sheena activated that switch in them through her over-giving and lack of boundaries. They did not behave the same way with other people, only with those that allowed it. I don't believe they were even conscious of their predatory behavior. Someone was giving them money so they kept taking it. **Read this twice: There are predators that are animalistic with anyone and everyone, and then there are**

normal people who take advantage of you because you allow it.

This tendency also comes from our evolutionary history. As a species, we have evolved to "conserve energy" whenever possible. Life was tough so our hunter-gatherer ancestors conserved energy wherever they could. So, if someone else showed up with food or other necessary things, they thought, "*Oh good, I can take this and not have to go out and risk my life.*" That "conserve energy switch" is the reason it's easy to "spoil" or turn otherwise good people into predators through over-giving and enabling. Yes, we are talking about a different type of predatory behavior but it's important to be aware of both types on your journey.

Evil, animalistic predators have the same kind of spidey senses that predators in the wild do. In some ways, all humans have the ability to sense things, albeit perhaps under their conscious awareness. Just like a lion or cheetah can smell its prey and use its animal instincts to go after the capture of their prey, so can human predators. Predators have confessed in many interviews their ability to sense trauma and low self-worth in their targets. They go after people who they can sense will be easy targets and typically come from broken or weak familial units! If you have ever found yourself thinking, *why do I attract such people into my life, do I have a sign on my back?* I want you to know that you do. It's an energy that people like us send out and their animalistic instincts can sniff it out.

Basic Babes are often targeted and used for their energy and life force. Self-Aware Barbies are targeted for their finances and other resources. Your only solution is to heal your over-giving, people-pleasing tendencies and not be a target any more. I have been fortunate enough to do this through inner work and facilitate the same for my students and clients. Your first line of defense is raising your consciousness IQ through gaining self-awareness and emotional control so you can no longer be manipulated.

Emotional Control

Most people are addicted to the same one or two emotional states. This is because emotions are highly addictive, and very potent chemical soups. Without self-awareness and grit, emotional addictions are very hard to break. If you were addicted to drugs, we could lock you in a rehab room and after a certain time, you would detox and be free of the drug addiction. Unfortunately, we can't do the same with emotional addictions. Wherever you go, your emotions are right there with you. There is no rehab room to lock you in for your addictions to suffering that lead you to seek out drama like bees to honey. You must decide and then learn to overcome these addictions through your sheer will and determination. Drama is the high you seek because of the human tendencies towards suffering. Drama isn't all entirely bad, but we need to place it back into our movies, plays, and outfits and not in our lives and relationships.

Since I gained emotional control, I have noticed a pattern with some people that I want to bring to your attention. Because I tend not to overreact or get caught up in the emotions of the moment, people having an emotional outburst might blame me for not being empathetic or harsh. At first, I was curious why they were saying that and closely examined my own behaviors and exact words and reactions. Honestly, I didn't do or say anything wrong. I was apologetic, validating their experience, without taking over their current emotional state. It has been interesting to see the reactions other people have to my emotional control. Some may start blaming you for what they are feeling, or try to drag you into their emotional world. The reason I couldn't be taken in their states was because I didn't see the problem as an actual problem in my world while acknowledging that they had a very different threshold for problems. My best advice is to validate what they are feeling without entangling with their emotions and let them figure it out. You can't control someone else's emotions at the end of the day and don't let them control yours either.

Here are my five steps to gaining emotional control over our addiction to suffering.

Step 1: Free Will and Seeing Everyone as Capable

None of the other tips I am sharing in this book worked for me until I understood this one, simple concept. If you want yourself to be loved, respected, and understood, you need to see everyone else as capable. Just like you are capable of figuring it out, being resourceful, showing up, doing the hard steps, and getting results, so are they. Yes, it's pretty frustrating to see other humans as fully capable when they don't see it in themselves. The truth is that they are conserving energy, yes, being lazy, because someone has always been available to bail them out.

I wholeheartedly believe in free will. This means I see all humans as fully capable of making good decisions for themselves. I see them as capable even before they see themselves as capable, and if needed, I give them the ability to prove it to themselves. This is why I confidently cut things off with my mom's family allowing them the grace to be capable of supporting themselves. There is absolutely no reason why whole generations of adult people need to depend on other people!

Every person on the planet has the right to choose how they wish to view life, what emotions they choose to run in their system, and what decisions they make as a result. When someone says to me, "*I have the right to be angry,*" I always agree. "*Yes, you have the right to be angry, but is that the right you want to exercise right now?*" You also have the right to not be angry.

Sure, I could have chosen to be angry about a whole lot of things, but I also have the right to choose something that serves me better, and that's what I decided to do. When you see people as capable, you don't jump in to solve their problems the minute they call you. You don't wire money over the minute someone is short on cash. Or drop everything and run to put out every fire they themselves have started. **Read this twice: Their urgency is not your priority.**

If you have the tendency to jump in and save everyone and then bitch and complain about it, that's on you, boo. Watch your own thought processes, emotions, and nervous system. What is it about YOU that has you jumping up and running to save everyone. The next time this happens, stop, feel, and respond slowly. You can be supportive to your family and friends without becoming everyone's sole life line. I am not saying never help anyone ever again. There is a big difference between helping out a friend in a bind versus enabling someone for a lifetime and never letting them figure things out for themselves. Helping someone feels good. Enabling someone always feels bad, causes resentment, and makes us feel used and depleted. Learn to recognize the difference.

Here is a script that may help you in those moments when someone calls in with yet another request: *"Oh, no, I'm so sorry you are going through this again. I'm sure you will figure it out in no time. I will say a prayer for your success"*

Be supportive without being a firefighter. See them as capable. Watch your own nervous system.

One question I always get from my students is, "*What if they get mad?*" And my response is always, "*Everyone has the right to their emotions.*" They are certainly allowed to get mad, sad, or whatever else. These are all normal human emotions. Feeling these emotions and then working through them are things all healthy human beings must learn to do. It is not your job to control other people's emotions. I can't even imagine what kind of shambles my life would be in right now if I worried about controlling other people's emotions.

Journal Prompts:

Is it hard for me not to jump in and save certain people, or perhaps everyone? Where does this come from?

What will happen if I don't help? What am I most afraid of? What are the core beliefs underneath this fear? Are these beliefs serving me?

What new beliefs do I need to embody to get over my over-giving and overdoing tendencies?

Step 2: Let it All Play Out

One thing that really helped me on the journey to re-wiring my brain for more peace and abundance is this concept I learned from Sheena. I noticed that when Sheena would encounter even the biggest and most scary of problems, she would wave her hand over her head and say, "*Let it all play out.*" And that was it. Of course, she would take the actions she needed to take. But she would take them with little to no emotional attachment to the outcome. This has been paradigm shifting for me and the thousands of my students who have learned to embody this mindset.

I honestly think this was Sheena's way of using the Law of Attraction without even realizing it. What I noticed when I started using the "let it play out" method, is that most of the situations I was seeing as "problems" resolved themselves with little to no help from me. In fact, they worked out better without my worried, anxious energy added to the mix! Most of the time, the perceived or "imaginary problems" didn't actually occur. And if they did, they played themselves out until they weren't a problem anymore. At other times, other people figured it out without me needing to help or save them. In fact, most things resolved themselves better without my tempering!

It took me a few months to rewire my brain to embody this concept, but it has saved my life. I say that only half jokingly. We all know stress is a huge contribution to illness. I didn't need to be making shit up and worrying about it when battling my autoimmune issues. My clients and students have also reported huge mental and energetic shifts from simply letting things play out.

It's important to remember that this doesn't mean that some action won't be required from you. But taking action laden with worry and anxiety is very different from taking action in faith that everything always works out for you. One feels very heavy and burdensome, while the other feels light and expansive. Try it the next time your brain tries to freak you out over something!

One thing I have realized is that most things that happened in my life not only didn't seem like problems later, they, in fact, turned into lessons with blessings. I am grateful for all of my life experiences because they shaped the woman that I am today. Realizing this has helped me not be too quick to judge things currently playing out in my life.

As a family, we have faced many "problems" that later turned out to be huge blessings. At the time they were happening, we were all very worried and scared. But even a year later, it all seemed like a huge blessing because of the lessons and changes that came from them. A lot of these events helped shape the very blessed and robust family we have today. So now when something happens, we aren't quick to jump and call it a "problem" or "huge disaster". We simply right-size the situation, count our blessings, and remind ourselves that we will be judging this as positive in the near future. So might as well do it now! Your attitude and mindset determines 90% of your life.

I stopped having problems because I stopped seeing things as problems. Don't judge what is happening now and let it play out. Chances are you will have a very different outcome of blessings than what you are able to see now anyways.

Side note: Sometimes friends or family members will get you invested in their made up problems. This usually starts with them future casting all of the bad things that "could" happen in the future. Here is my script for that: *"I don't solve problems that haven't happened yet. We will deal with it, when and if it happens."*

Journal Prompts:

What am I currently tempering with that I simply need to "let play out?"

___

___

___

Where was I quick to judge something as a problem because I couldn't see all of its gifts and blessings?

___

___

___

Step 3: Starve Out Drama

Starving out drama means that drama literally dies when it lands on you. You become the anti-venom of drama. This is where a lot of my students start seeing their own play into the drama they claim someone else was creating. I want you to start thinking of and treating drama like it's a parasite. It attacks your consciousness and zaps your life force energy. The thing with drama is that it needs a carrier to live on and spread. Someone has to house it, feed it, and transport it around. Like all life, it loves to expand and grow. Hopping from human to human and getting bigger and bigger in the meantime. Like vampires, it needs permission to enter your home, which means you can literally refuse entry! You have been in control this whole time.

Once drama is invited in and makes contact with you, notice your own tendency to spread it. You talk it over with your mother, best friend, husband, and then make passive aggressive posts about it on social media. Why on earth would someone who claims to hate drama prolong it in this way?

Here are some examples of this. Someone cuts you off in traffic and gives you the finger. Feel what you are feeling and then drop it. Let it go. No need to post on Facebook, and tell everyone else that will listen. It's over. You are safe now. The lunatic didn't infect you. The whole thing lasted maybe two minutes. The rest of it is you prolonging it by telling the whole world about it and thus keeping it alive in your nervous system. **Starve it out technique:** Feel what you are feeling, count your blessings, so in this case that this lunatic is now gone, and keep it moving.

If someone adds you to an angry chain of text messages, don't respond. Tell them you lost your phone if you run into them later. No need to screenshot the messages and send them to your sister and other friends. No need to go off to your husband about how insensitive people are these days. Why bring that drama to your other relationships that have nothing to do with all of this. **Starve it out technique:** Remove yourself and/or block them and move on with your beautiful life.

If you know something will trigger your mom or sister, don't call them and tell them about it. Act like a grown-up, independent, sovereign being that doesn't have to report back every single thing to people. I can't tell you how many of my clients I have caught doing this. They would get on sessions with me complaining about all the things their mom/friend/sister said to them about their new career or dating preferences. When I would ask how the conversation got started, the answer was always, "*Oh, well I called and told her.*" Ahhh, who is the drama queen here?

Why invite drama in and then be upset that it showed up? Because in some ways we are all addicted to suffering as previously discussed. The good news is that you can choose not to be at any given time. The minute drama enters your field, it's buried. That's it. It took me about a month or so to implement this into my life but everything changed when I did. I thought I was attracting people who loved drama. Turns out,

I was also addicted to it! I was the one carrying and spreading it!

In my mid-twenties, I had a friend who was a huge magnet to drama. Drama loved her like they were soul mates. She would call me at all hours of the day and night. Sometimes even at 2 or 3 am. And I would spend hours listening to her. We would dissect all her issues with the men of the week. The issues with her parents, siblings, and co-workers. It never ended. Being her friend was honestly a whole full time, unpaid position. I didn't even realize how much time and energy she was using up. All of our lunches or dinners were consumed with her latest drama. I was just there to listen and pay.

And then suddenly, one day she moved away. She continued calling for a bit but soon we drifted apart. I was amazed at how much more time, energy, and space I suddenly had. People started commenting on how much more relaxed I looked and asked if I had a facial. I had so much more time suddenly and started contemplating my next moves. Who I wanted to really be in life. That was the year I manifested my husband. Let this be a lesson in emotional energy. When we use it up for drama, we have less to use to create our dream life.

Journal Prompts:

Where in my life am I inviting drama in?

How am I carrying and spreading it around?

Where can I let drama simply starve itself out?

Step 4: Outsource Your Problems

"*What would happen if you made this next bold move in your business?*" There was a brief silence on the other end where I could almost hear the wheels turning. I was on a coaching call with a client who had her first few six figure months after joining my CEO Boss Queen business course but was suddenly feeling stuck or "blocked" as she referred to it.

"*I could get cancer, or get sued.*" Ahhh, there it was! The fear of success or "container issue" as I refer to it in my work (more on that in a later chapter).

"*Well, what does a successful and resourceful woman like you usually do when you have a problem, let's say a toothache?*" I asked her.

"*I go to the dentist?*" I could sense it was dropping in, but clarified to make my point and get the "OMG I get it" reaction I so love to awaken. "*Yes, exactly, so if you got cancer, you would go to the doctor, find a cure, monetize it, and make more money than you can even imagine right now. If you get sued, well then there are lawyers who love that sort of thing.*" Not sure which I heard first, her sigh of relief or laughter!

"*OMG! I will figure it out!! There is always support, I don't have to do it all right now or alone!*" She practically screamed back in excitement.

Yes, babe. You will figure it all out. There is always support and solutions are always available to us. There is absolutely no reason to be afraid of taking the next steps in our journey. No matter what your primitive, "trying to keep you so safe, it's cute" brain tells you otherwise. Believe it or not there are people out there who specialize in solving your exact real or imaginary problems. In fact, it may also be their zone of genius.

Instead of worrying about a water leak, you simply hire a plumber and trust him to do his job. Toothache? That's the dentist's domain. On coaching calls with the world's most brilliant top 1% women, I often remind them that not all of their problems are to be solved by them. So, worrying about them makes no sense. Stay in your lane and zone of genius.

A lot of this worrying stems from what is referred to as Imposter Syndrome. Imposter Syndrome is a form of "container issue" where you doubt your worthiness and think you will be found out as some kind of a "fake" or "imposter" for sharing your light with the world. When these women are having a container issue, their mind instantly goes into creating these horrible "what if" scenarios.

What if I get cancer?

What if I get stalked or someone threatens me?

Here is my reply. Anyone, anywhere can get cancer. That is just a reality of life. You living and sharing your brilliantly sacred light with the world isn't going to cause cancer. In fact, there are many people online sharing their stories of how living authentically and sharing their light actually cured their cancer! And even if you did get cancer, you are one badass resourceful chick who will find the best medical and metaphysical team on your side, get cured, and then probably use your wisdom to help others. You see how this works, it's all happening for you.

And people who aren't living their best lives, creating massive change on the planet with their light and work have these things happen to them as well. You can get threatened or stalked at your job or gym, unfortunately. There are lawyers, doctors, police officers, private detectives, judges, and a host of other professionals ready to help take our problems off our hands. None of these "not happened yet" scenarios should scare you into not being YOU.

You are always divinely protected. Your spiritual guides, Angels, and non-physical ancestors have your back at all times.

Another solution is to hand over your problems to your higher self or the Universe. This has worked wonders for me. I simply hand over my problem to God and ask for a clear sign on how I can support God in solving this problem. Here is an exercise that has helped many of my students:

Homework:

Take a sheet of notebook paper and fold it in half vertically. On one side write down the words: **God's job**. On the other side write down: **My job.**

Now whenever you find yourself swimming in problems, write down what is God's job and what is your job. Here are some examples:

God's Job:

Figure out the solutions and send me signs on which actions to take if any.

My Job:

Keep the faith.

Take aligned action trusting that God has a plan.

Feel good.

Journal Prompts:

What do I currently worry about that is not my job?

____

____

____

How can I properly outsource those "problems" to others who love solving those exact problems?

____

____

____

Step 5: Upgrade Your Problems

This concept has ruffled a few feathers every time I have talked about it. However, I believe it's worth discussing here. In our lower consciousness stages, we tend to classify a long list of things as "problems." It could be anything from car related issues to spending hours decoding text messages to see what your date actually meant. What if none of these were actually problems in your world? What if these things didn't even register in your consciousness at all?

Here is the assignment: Raise the bar to what you consider a problem.

For inspiration, let me share the list of things I actually consider a problem in my life. As I do with a lot of things in life, I look to evolution to determine how to best approach this for myself. This doesn't mean I am judging other people's problems as some people seem to assume. I don't concern myself with that sort of thing, I believe everyone has a right to their own problems. I just choose to elevate mine.

Things I consider actual problems:

- Loss of life or immediate threat to life (for me or loved one)
- Inability to find immediate shelter
- Immediate food insecurity (actual scarcity)
- Illness (for me or loved one)

As you can see this is a very short list. Everything else I consider a distraction to me actually living in God's flow. Here is how I deal with imaginary problems: I never waste any energy or resources on "problems" that haven't occurred yet. I have wired myself not to worry about the future. If it hasn't happened yet, why waste emotional energy on it? I reframe things others may consider problems. Missed flight? The Universe is rerouting me to a better one. Running late? God is protecting me.

Everything else is life playing itself out in my opinion. It may even be the Universe rearranging itself in my favor. That's why I'm not quick to judge the present moment. Now being human we do enjoy having some fun problems to solve. Some people apparently love math for example, I call these upgraded problems.

The mental and emotional energy that is freed up from no longer dealing with perceived problems and self created drama can now be put to good use. Use that energy to improve your lifestyle. Go bigger and bolder in your career. Take up some creative skills. Create the upgraded "problem" of earning more money, learning new investment opportunities, traveling to exotic places and more, taking up a new fitness routine. These are the kind of upgraded, luxurious challenges that put your brain to good use and create more excitement and bliss in your life. I enjoy my drama in my movies and my outfits. I have come to realize that most of my problems in my Basic Babe and Self-Aware Barbie days were imaginary. Not only did I not need to solve them, but as I evolved, I would just outgrow them.

Journal Prompts:

What do I consider actual problems in my life?

____

____

____

What am I currently removing emotional energy from?

____

____

____

What are my new, upgraded, elevated "problems" that I enjoy investing time and energy into?

____

____

____

CHAPTER *Five* THE HAVING IT ALL BLUEPRINT

At 21, I got into real estate with my mother. She had gotten her real estate license and was doing extremely well. In fact, she became the number one seller in the office out of 200 agents her first year. I was at university at the time and decided to see if I could learn from her. I immediately started making more money than I had ever seen in my life. I then decided to try my hand at purchasing investment properties, remodeling, and then flipping them to make extra money like some of our clients were doing. I was making multiple six figures a year the following year, while going to school! However, no matter how much money I made, I could never keep any of it for long.

I didn't realize this at the time but my parents' money habits and behaviors had been ingrained into my psyche. Even though I always despised the fact that they were so bad with money, I became exactly like them! Not only had I inherited their toxic money habits, but I was also massively into people-pleasing and over-giving, exactly like them! I kept thinking it was everyone else's fault for not honoring my boundaries and putting me in uncomfortable situations. The funny thing is that I would stop associating with certain people who were triggering people-pleasing and over giving in me, only to have someone else show up acting exactly in the same ways.

I didn't know this at the time of course, but I was being prepared to heal those triggers, that is why they kept showing up! Our triggers will keep repeating themselves until we actually heal them. Avoiding them just keeps prolonging the misery. We are triggered when something in our environment hits upon a sore spot in our psyche. It's your subconscious saying *something needs to be explored and released here.*

When exploring your triggers, there are two concepts that I have found to be life changing. Your core beliefs and your personal values. Not only did these concepts heal my past, but they also helped me stay protected from all levels of predators. The inner work I am about to share is foundational, don't just gloss over it. If you want to truly recreate yourself from the inside out, spend some time on this chapter.

Core Beliefs

Core beliefs are unconscious datasets that dictate our thoughts, feelings, mindsets, and behaviors. They dictate what we see or filter out as options for ourselves. As you can imagine, they are very important! This must be addressed before proceeding with any other inner work or taking anyone's advice. I can give you an exact script of success and it won't do you much good if it hits up against your core beliefs.

In my real estate example, the reason I couldn't save money despite making so much was because of the core beliefs I had inherited from my parents. Core beliefs run behind the scenes in our subconscious. So even though my conscious mind wanted to save money, have investments, and build wealth to become a millionaire, my subconscious mind had other plans. Core beliefs are the ultimate gate keeper. Most of our core beliefs are programmed in childhood (some even in utero!) and therefore we are not aware of them. Unless you actively take the time to explore yours and update them to match your current lifestyle goals, the old ones will be running the show!

My core belief at this time of my life was *I can make money but it's hard to keep it.* As you can see, with a core belief like that, any attempts at saving money will be sabotaged by your subconscious mind. I used to spend so much time watching Suze Orman and learning about saving money. I opened up many savings accounts, CDs and God knows what else to try to save money but nothing worked. Some "emergency" always showed up and the money was spent quickly. You can't live life past your core beliefs.

Your core beliefs shape your identity and will need to be examined and visited and revisited many times throughout your life. If your identity doesn't match where you are headed, your subconscious won't let you go there. This is why we self-sabotage our growth. For example, one of Sheena's core beliefs was that she is financially responsible for her entire extended family and even their extended families. Every decision she made was a function of this core belief running behind the scenes like a computer program. This is why she wasn't even available for a conversation about this topic with her own daughter! The good news is that you can program and reprogram your subconscious with any core belief at any time in your life. Most people don't do this because they don't even realize it's an option!

Here are some of my updated and current core beliefs. These are the ones I choose for myself and have embodied intentionally.

Everyone is capable and fully responsible for their own life, finances, decisions, emotions, and happiness.

The Universe wants to give me all of my desires.

Being happy and wealthy is my birthright and my gift to humanity.

I get to win in every situation and so does everyone else.

Everything is always working out for me. Even if I can't see it at that exact moment.

It is not my job to interfere with someone else's learning process.

Everyone has free will and is fully capable of co-creating a beautiful life with the Divine.

I get to have money, keep money, spend money, and grow money. Money is a renewable resource.

Okay so now it's time for some homework. It's your turn to write out your core beliefs. If you are unsure what your core beliefs are, here are two options for you.

Option one: Look at your current life. Core beliefs leave very obvious clues. Poverty core beliefs lead to scarcity showing up in your life and finances. Lack of worthiness core beliefs lead to nasty relationships and charging your worth. In my private and group coaching, I have helped thousands of people figure out and change their core beliefs.

But honestly, I have found an easier way over the years.

Option two: Regardless of what your current core beliefs are, you can decide to upgrade them.

With option two, there is no need to figure out what the current core beliefs are. Remember that I believe we get to win in every situation, so no point in getting stuck in any exercise or process. Here is my simple yet potently effective 6 step process to recoding your core beliefs. Use the process every time a negative though, fear, or doubt pops up as you are moving towards your desires.

End the Struggle Inner Work 6 Step Process:

1. What is the distortion that my mind is creating? What is the old story? Is this ultimately true?
2. Say the Surrender Prayer. *"Dear God, please help me release the distortions and lies my mind is creating. I am willing to see things differently. Please help me see and accept new, upgraded, high vibration realities."*
3. What is the NEW, Upgraded Truth or Belief system that I am ready to embody? Write out the new story for yourself in your journal.

4. Now close your eyes and spend 2-3 minutes imaging yourself living out the new story. Notice all the details. How are you carrying yourself? How are you speaking? Do you move and/or sound differently? What are you wearing? Is your energy and vibration different? Notice and record this as a movie so you can play it in your mind often.
5. Affirm new beliefs by saying "I Am…" statements with as much feeling as possible. The feeling part is essential! Repetition and High Emotion is what programs the subconscious mind. The higher the emotion, the less repetition is needed. Here are some statements to get you started.

   "I Am Worthy."

   "I Am Enough."

   "I Am Wealthy."

   "I Am Healthy."

   "I Am the Reciprocal for Healthy Divine Union."
6. Repeat the new statements with feelings of new core beliefs millions of times until the subconscious memorizes new truths and belief systems. Remember, the higher the emotional state when you feel into your new core beliefs, the less repetition is needed.

Beware of the ego's trick to get you distracted as you set out to shift your identity by embracing new core beliefs. This may show up as: Bringing up unnecessary questions that don't really need to be answered. These questions will simply be outgrown with your new beliefs. Manifesting drama, toxic situations, and people back into your reality. Simply don't engage. Just observe and let it pass. Another one I have seen is getting sick and not being able to do the inner work! Even if this happens, keep reciting the affirmations and prayer Another one is making things seem harder than they are.

Repeat: "*Inner work gets to be EASY AND FUN!!*"

Releasing Shame and Guilt

Prayer: "*Dear God, Universe, Angels, I release all guilt and shame. Please transmute all distortions into love and free me from all mental and energetic constraints.*"

Inner Work Prompt: Write down "I feel guilty for.." and "I feel shame when...". Then write down the limiting beliefs that accompany that guilt or shame. Work through those LIES using the six-step process given above.

Choose new, more empowering beliefs for yourself!! There are always deeper layers to guilt and shame and once you can work through and reframe them, they no longer mean anything to you.

Affirmations:

"*I am now free.*"

"*I am now healed from all shame and guilt.*"

"*I now release all shame and guilt.*"

This simple process will start to unravel old neural pathways and build new ones matching your new way of being. It also expands your nervous system into holding more higher states of being.

Here is another Core Beliefs exercise that I love!

Set a 10-minute timer on your phone.

Then without lifting your pen off your paper, keep writing the following statement and finishing it with your new empowering core beliefs.

I choose to know and believe...

For example: "*I choose to know and believe that everything is always working out for me, even when I can't see it.*"

"*I choose to know and believe that I am healed and whole now.*"

"*I choose to know and believe that my desires are God's plan.*"

"*I choose to know and believe that my existence is a gift to humanity.*"

I do these exercises every morning and it has been life changing!

Personal Values

Personal values are decisions you make once and automate forever, or at least until you decide to upgrade them again. I like to keep my mind light and free to make the more creative decisions in my life. You know the kind of things that actually level up my life and help others from my overflow. I decide once and automate most of life as personal values. Keep in mind that personal values are not things you say, but things you live by.

I think my personal values have helped hugely in keeping myself safe from people with bad intentions. Before I started doing inner work, I had to gauge every person and situation and see how I wanted to proceed. There were times when I would decide that

I was going to focus on myself before helping anyone else and then someone would show up and seem urgent (for them at least) and I would once again go off running helping them. It always ended with no appreciation and even complaints of how I didn't help enough, leaving me resentful and mad at myself for not honoring my boundaries.

Personal values combined with a change in core beliefs was a huge paradigm shift. Personal values helped me set parameters for myself and "decide once" how I was going to handle all future requests. Having values as guiding posts made it so much easier to say no and stick with my preset boundaries.

Here are some of my personal values.

Sukoon. Sukoon is the Arabic word for deep inner peace and enlightenment. Peace is truly my highest value. I place this even above my family because without inner peace I won›t be bringing my best self to them.

Freedom. I don't like being told what to do or when to do it. Rules make me feel suffocated. Because of this, I have placed freedom as one of my highest values.

God & Faith. My faith in God is another high value. Things that don't align with this can't be in my life.

Personal Growth. I believe I came to this planet to expand the consciousness of the collective. When I grow, the morphogenetic field grows. So, I show up and keep learning and expanding daily as if it was my career. And therefore I made it my career to keep myself in check! LOL

Family. My children and husband come first. Before all others. I will never help someone else at the expense of my family or myself.

Fun. Ease. I refuse to do anything that's not fun and easy. And if it isn't, I make it fun and easy. In fact, many say that making things fun and easy is my gift.

My core beliefs and personal values make decision making really easy for me. I don't have to decide on the whim when a new opportunity or life path presents itself. Does this thing match my personal values? If it passes the test, it's a hell yes! If it doesn't it's an immediate, "no, thank you."

So, let's put it all together using me as an example. Let's say a friend who always manages to get themselves into all kinds of situations shows up to my door asking for help. She needs a place to stay once again and was hoping she can stay with me. The last time she did this, it was hell for me and my family for 3 whole weeks when it was supposed to be only for "a few days." After three weeks she went back to her boyfriend and made me look like the bad guy for keeping her apart from her man! So, what do I do?

The old Mina, with a different set of core beliefs and lack of personal values would have been very upset but still said yes. Later she would have bitched and moaned to everyone that would listen while continuing to bend her boundaries, putting her family in uncomfortable situations, and continually saying yes when she really needed to say no! Moving her friend in would have soon led to cooking and cleaning for her, driving her around, listening to her friend complain about her boyfriend for hours every day, and entertaining and babysitting her kids. Putting aside the needs of her own and her family's well-being. Does this remind you of the childhood pattern Mina herself lived through with her parents moving in people into their home? Do you see how generational curses function and play out?

Let's examine what the new and leveled up Mina would do. According to her new core beliefs, she sees everyone as having free will over their decisions and the ability and capability of figuring things out. She also believes that interfering with someone else's learning process is not her job. New Mina's personal values say that sukoon, freedom, family, and faith are important ways of living her life. Does helping her friend help her stay in sukoon, keep her freedom, honor her family and her faith? The answer is no. Based on this, she empathizes with her friend, and lets her know she trusts that her friend can figure it out. Knowing that bailing out someone else's mistakes by moving them in is not necessary, she can choose to help in her aligned ways only if she desires and it matches her values.

Here is a sample script.

"*Oh no, babe, I'm so sorry you are going through this again. It must be so hard for you to be in this situation. I know that the Universe has something amazing in store for you and you will get yourself out of this situation. I am unable to open my home at this time, however I can…*"

"*Give you money for a night at the hotel.*" or "*Drive you to a family member's house.*" (only give the last bit of options if you do want to help in some way and it won't make you resentful. Someone else's urgency is not your priority. I only help when and if it feels good to me and comes from my overflow, not from my depletion.)

Here is the most important thing I want you to take from core beliefs and personal values: They must be the same for everyone in every situation. This means that your core beliefs and personal values are not up for negotiation! This is the part that makes it a part of your identity and not something anyone can mess with or manipulate you around. If people figure out that your personal values go out the door under x and y conditions, they will bring those conditions to you and try to negotiate. If everyone knows that moving in with me is never an option, under any circumstances, then it's never even a discussion.

I have learned these lessons the hard way. Today in my life, I enjoy full peace and freedom and no one is expecting anything from me. Before I had developed these beliefs and values, someone was always trying to hack their way into my home and pockets. I had family members and friends faking accidents, pregnancies, heart attacks, and God knows what else. Just like they did with Sheena for her entire life. Once everyone figured out all I am good for is calling 911 for you, the shenanigans stopped.

Predators and manipulators bank on you bending the rules just this one time. Making exceptions for their extreme situations, dire emergencies, and dashing good looks and cuteness. Nope. The values are what the values are and they stay the same for everyone. I have seen women in the dating world bend the rules for the "cute guys" that they are into but uphold them for men they find average or are not into. This strategy always seems to get them into all kinds of situations. Decide once how you will behave in all situations and then stick with that no matter who shows up.

One example of this from my personal life is personal online donation accounts such as GoFundMe. These are basically donation raising platforms where anyone can set up an account and start collecting donations. My husband and I decided on what values we have around charity and giving early on in our marriage. Especially considering my triggers on my family giving at the expense of themselves and their own well-being. Our values are that we only donate to people and charities we personally know and where we know all of the funds will be used in the way it is claimed. So, if a company uses 98% of the funds claimed to go to children for marketing instead, that doesn't match our values. We would rather hand the money to the family directly.

Years later, we started getting requests from family members and friends to donate to their GoFundMe accounts for people we didn't know and had zero confidence that the money would actually go where it was claimed. I have actually seen people using donation money collected for "health emergencies" for vacations and dining out! So, does donating to these accounts fit our core beliefs and personal values? Absolutely not. Regardless of who shows up asking for that donation, we said no, and eventually people got the memo that we don't donate to people we don't personally know. There is nothing that can be said or done to make us bend our values in this area. Decided once and automated.

Lesson: Our core beliefs and personal values are automations that help us decide once. Core beliefs are stored in the subconscious and need to be updated as we evolve and grow to match our new identity. Personal values are decisions you make once and then filter all future options through. They make your life streamlined and cohesive and since they are unbendable and the same for all people, it keeps manipulators and users away.

Journal Prompts:

What are my current core beliefs? Are they serving me?

Do my current core beliefs need to be updated to match the new identity I am creating for myself?

What are my current personal values? How will these help me decide once and automate?

How will I uphold these decisions for everyone?

Expand Your Container

I can't end this chapter without talking about container work! If you have been a part of my work for a while, then you have heard me use this word many times. This may be a good time for us to define the concept for those that are new to this world. There are two ways I use the word *container*. The first way is to describe the masculine containment of the feminine. The structure of the riverbed holding the feminine flow of the water is one example. A literal bowl holding the soup is another one. Your husband planning a romantic evening for you is also an example of a masculine container for you to enjoy your evening in your feminine energy.

The second way the word container is used in my work is to describe the emotional set point or subconscious edges of what we will allow into our experience. If you are used to being lower middle class, and win the lottery, your "container" won't allow you to keep that money. This is exactly why lottery winners have such a hard time keeping their winnings. About 95% of lottery winners lose the money and wish they hadn't won it. They didn't have enough time, space, and awareness to expand their container because of the sudden nature of their wealth.

Our internal containers are also why most humans are addicted to suffering. That has been such a huge timeline in our human existence that even with our newfound abundance, we still are trapped inside the smaller, tighter, more constrictive, old container. All of us must expand our container to allow ourselves to feel safe even if we perceive imaginary wild animals hunting us as once were true. We must expand our container to feel abundant even when our emotional collective set point is set to scarcity of food.

In simple terms, your "container" is your energetic and emotional set point of how good you will allow your life to get.

Some people may have a larger container or capacity to receive love but a very small container for money. Others may manifest money very easily but sabotage love and keep going back to the same familiar loser type they have been dating since high school. If you want to have it good in all areas of importance to you, you must expand and stabilize your container! Upgrade the human emotional body, energetic capacity, and nervous system.

How do you know if you are having a "container issue"?

- What you desire seems too good to be true.
- You sabotage it as soon as it manifests.
- You manifest the desire but some other area of your life quickly attracts problems.

You find yourself thinking of bad things that can happen right after a big win or amazing moment.

How to Expand your Container

The first thing I suggest is to change your core beliefs regarding each area of your life especially when you are manifesting something new and different in that area.

Get comfortable being uncomfortable for a while when something new is manifested in your life. Anything that is an upgrade to your current energetic set point will be uncomfortable by default.

Expand your ability to hold more joy and blessings in your nervous systems using my exclusive formula shared in my Femm Fortune Container Course:

Container Formula: Depth + Time = More

Depth is how deeply you allow something to penetrate your senses, and therefore re-regulate your nervous system. Your nervous system programs anything that you do with high emotion for longer than 20 minutes or with enough repetition. If you can really, deeply feel into something and allow your nervous system either enough time or repetition, it will start to upregulate to a new container. In the above formula, depth represents high emotion and how deeply you feel that emotion in your nervous system, and time represents how long and how many times. More represents the expansion of your container.

I have given the container a scale of 1 to 10 to help my students better track their progress, with 10 being you feel utter and sheer ecstatic joy and it just is a part of who you are and what you allow for new manifestations. One is you completely going into rock bottom and self-sabotage in that area of your life if something new shows up.

For example, if you receive a compliment and immediately follow it up with a "*oh, this old thing,*" it reveals your small container for receiving compliments. And since containers impact more than one area, chances are you also have trouble receiving in other areas of your life.

So, let's say you receive compliments at a 3.

The next step is to try and feel more into the compliment then next time you receive it. Hold that tendency to want to brush it off immediately. Can you feel into the compliment at a 2.5 next time for a few seconds longer each time? The more conscious you are and the more repetition with high emotion there is, the more your container will expand. Small moves are better when it comes to container work then trying to move too quickly and self-sabotaging right back.

The final step in your container work is to normalize your new blessings. Make them "no big deal" by letting them be a part of your identity and not something you have once in a while or as a fluke. I do this by changing my core beliefs, allowing my new manifestations to become the new normal of my reality but engaging with it often, and by affirming…

"This just is… It's no big deal. Mina Irfan simply gets to have this and more."

Homework:

In what areas of your life do you need a larger container?

What is the current number from 1 to 10 for this container?

What are the steps you will take to expand your container just a little bit more?

The Have it All Ideal Blueprint for Feminine Women

I believe in brutal honesty, acceptance, and responsibility with myself and I extend that brutal honesty to those I love. Evolutionarily speaking, women have evolved to be more agreeable and evolved to tend and befriend over telling the truth in fear of hurting feelings and ruffling feathers. This is something I have had to work through. I pride myself in giving you the same advice I would give my daughter. I am tired of women lying to each other so as not to hurt feelings and withholding information that has the potential to offer the kind of guidance that would change someone's life.

Here is the truth, women are vastly different from men. We have very different timelines and work best by acknowledging and working with our different seasons of life. I believe that every single woman can have everything they desire and prioritize in life but not necessarily all at once. The truth is that most of us simply don't have the nervous system and emotional container to have it all at once anyways. Having it all is a beautiful journey of a lifetime. As a woman, I want you to look at you having it all as an 85-100 year journey split into beautiful seasons of life. Honoring your biological and psychological needs and timelines in each season.

My daughter is nine years old at the time of this writing and what follows is the feminine life blueprint that I am teaching her as all mothers do in my culture. I share it with you here in hopes of inspiration, fully understanding that life isn't always perfect or entirely on our plan. Having a blueprint can at least get our juices flowing and make us more intentional on our life plan. This is the same blueprint modern women of my culture follow, so it's been tried and true and works really well. I made the decision to share this sacred blueprint passed down from women to women in my culture with you after holding space for tens of thousands of students from all over the world. Girls and women are so currently confused and misled on this space in the world. We all desire motherly nurturing, protection, and guidance but everyone is too afraid of political correctness to give it to us.

What I am about to share with you goes against our current culture so much, I almost decided not to share it. I know this is going to massively trigger some women so I shared this with my YouTube audience first. About 99.9% of women received this information well, the .1% that were initially triggered came back and thanked me for being brutally honest. Many decided to plan their lives accordingly after hearing this information. **As you read this section know this: It is never too late to manifest your desires. Knowledge is truly power. I would rather the truth trigger you than a lie coddle you. There are always exceptions to every rule and not everything I am about to share will apply to everyone.**

It has been shocking for me to sit through coaching call after coaching call with women in their late 30s or early 40s just painfully realizing that they can no longer freeze their eggs or have babies. What bothered me the most about each of these scenarios was that my clients truly didn't know there was a deadline for women to have babies. This didn't make sense to me because I had been given this information when I was a little girl and had planned my life accordingly. Upon investigating this further with my tens of thousands of students and hundreds of thousands on YouTube, I was even more surprised at what I learned.

Not only are western women not given this information, they are often given the complete opposite imagery. Modern women are taught to prioritize their careers over their deepest desires and biology. We grow up in a culture with celebrities having babies well into their forties. They never reveal the full picture behind the scenes of what it took for these celebrities to actually get pregnant and the risks they took to have their babies later in life. My students had no idea that the rate of childbirth complications and birth defects goes up in relation to the age of the mother! They were never given this vital information so they could decide how to plan their life.

Armed with this knowledge, my students now have the option to create a beautiful life experience for themselves and make the best decisions for themselves and their families. Choice often requires knowledge. I encourage you to go and do some research on the cons and pros of having children in your 20s vs your 30s and making the best, informed decision for yourself.

If you are a feminine essence being like me, you truly value and prioritize relationships and connection. Even if you have been wounded or conditioned out of it, deep down you still value it. The current western programming has conditioned you to believe that relationships and parenting are not only very hard, but also dangerous, unnatural and something you have the choice to disregard. It doesn't take you far to look at what this has done to women's mental and physical health and society. Homo sapiens evolved as social creatures in families and extended tribes. Men are designed to hunt, protect, and provide. Women are designed to gather, nurture, love, have babies, and nest. Our biology and identity are tied to these roles we have played for millions of years. Take that away and we have a generation of lost and sick people.

Here is the 5 Seasons Blueprint I have followed and am also teaching my daughter.

Well-Rounded Skill Sets Era

Dating for Marriage Era

Marriage, Romance, and Inner Work Era

Baby-Making and Mothering Era

Wealthy Woman Era

Well-Rounded Skill Sets Era: From the ages of teen until you graduate from university, your priority should be education, acquiring life skills, and healing. There is absolutely no point in having a boyfriend or engaging in tons of drama with boys or female friendships at this stage. If you must have friends, stick with the type that prioritizes what you prioritize. Ditch them immediately if they cause trouble. You are a woman with a plan. Don't let them derail it. The decisions you make in this phase will make or break your future. Yes, I believe anything can rise from the ashes of any situation, but burning down only to rebuild yourself is an utter waste of time. Give yourself a head start by becoming allergic to anything that doesn't match your priorities at this time.

Your assignment in this era: Learn, Learn, Learn. Learn various skills that don't necessarily "go with each other." This is the difference between information and wisdom. Learn the various religions, how to cook, how the human body works, learn psychology, math, art, and all the other things that interest you. Also take this time to learn about yourself. Use this time to become a student of life and start developing your personal values. Notice the things that are the most important to you by observing others keenly. Become curious on what people around you do and how it affects their life. Start asking yourself important questions like: Do you value freedom, peace, security? Do you want a quiet life at home with some adventure, or lots of adventure with some quiet time at home?

While other women are wasting time engaging in unnecessary drama with worthless friendships and being traumatized with multiple fake boyfriend and girlfriend relationships, you will be laying down a plan of success. It may be hard to go against the grain right now, but you will thank me later when you see the damage these women create in their life, things you don't need to heal from. You will have your dignity, sanity, and peace. Use this time to join some more well rounded, traditional circles, even if you don't agree with everything they say, it will help you keep balance with the culture's anti-family programming.

If you had a difficult childhood, use this time to do your inner work. Read books, go to therapy, listen to older, embodied, successful people from various walks of life. But only the ones that have your dream life. Listening to the wrong people can greatly influence our psyche and create lots of doubt in our minds. Another thing to be mindful of in this stage is to retain your femininity. Some women can start losing this part of them even as early as high school, but definitely college. Stay away from feminist agendas. Women have won their rights in the western world now, at this point it's only a bunch of people addicted to suffering. None of us are perfect, but remember that when you heal, your womb won't pass down trauma to your future babies.

One of the things research has found is that western people tend to be more wired for masculine success and individualism. This is one of the reasons relationships are so difficult in the western cultures. In eastern culture, people tend to be wired more for community, connection, and relationships. Of course, there will be individual differences between people in every culture, but these studies looked at culture norms as a whole. Having had access to both western and eastern culture, and having struggled with losing my relationship "brain", I can attest to this personally. In my coaching practice, I have helped tens of thousands of women activate their femininity and rewire their brain for relationships. I will teach you how to do this in a later section.

Any jobs or career you take on during this stage should be something that you can either leave entirely or is flexible enough to prioritize dating, marriage, and babies in the near future. Use this time to become financially literate in both masculine and feminine ways of manifesting, investing, growing and attracting money. Since you are already a student in this stage, learn to prioritize your spending for things that are really aligned with your values. Remembering that your financial situation will keep growing and evolving and you don't have to figure it all out for yourself.

Dating for Marriage Era: After university, I want you to focus on dating for marriage, if marriage is on your life plan. Many women make the mistake of going after a career first. This not only puts them more into their masculinity, but it also changes the brain patterns from connection and love to achievement and individualism. Dating does not mean sleeping with men or becoming a girlfriend. You will learn more about a new way of dating for marriage in the next chapter. The man you choose should have very similar values to you. He doesn't have to have the same hobbies or interests as much as the same life values. Choose someone with a growth mindset so you can continue to grow young with him. Remember that this man will learn, evolve, and grow just like you. He doesn't have to have it all or be it all at once either.

Your assignment in this era: Rotational dating for marriage. You are not to choose a man based on your chemical responses of the moment. Chemistry fades, love grows. Look at him as someone you will do the remaining seasons of life with. Will he make a great friend, husband, father, and support network for your family and community? Is he someone who values family, traditions, gender roles, and marriage? The three most important things you can look for in your husband are similar values, growth mindset, and family background (this will reveal how much trauma he is carrying). Also notice if he is in the right phase to be able to provide for you and your future children. Ability and willingness to provide are an important indicator of male health as long as all the other boxes mentioned above match as well. You may have to choose someone a few years older than you to get someone more settled in life. I believe a healthy age gap is 3-7 years. Of course, you can choose someone your own age but then be prepared to help him build a little before you are able to have babies and stay at home with them.

Do not marry someone you have extreme chemistry with. Females should not choose mates based on emotions and feelings. Even the females in the animal kingdom know and understand this. Human females are the only ones that seem to have forgotten. Men choose mates based on emotions and attraction. You should choose based on the things we just discussed. Of course, we want to be attracted to our partner but this should not be the leading criteria. Whatever you do, do not sleep with him before marriage!! Our hormones are designed to filter out any red flags or serious character flaws after we sleep with someone. This helped nature ensure that two parents would be available for any children that resulted from that union. In the next chapter, I will teach you how to create a love list to attract your ideal match.

Marriage, Romance, and Inner Work Era: This is the era of weddings, honeymoons, romance, and inner work. If you choose wisely, your partner will trigger the hell out of you after the honeymoon period is over. This is actually a really great sign. Marriage is the most important test of your emotional and psychological healing. Everything and anything that needs to be healed will now rise up to the surface to be soothed and healed. We actually choose our partners subconsciously knowing they will help us heal our womb wounds and conditioning. Relationships are the closest resemblance to our birth families. This is why the wounds that occurred in childhood have the greatest chance of being healed in marriage. You aren't truly healed until you can have a healthy marriage.

Your assignment in this era: Decide that divorce is off the table and that you both are committed to loving and growing together. Decide on gender roles for this season of your life, remembering that you can change and evolve things in other seasons as needed. Take time to learn about each other, have fun, grow, learn, and help each other heal. Become each other's safe space for friendship, family, faith, and healing. Become dependent on each other, give and receive. Allow your life to intertwine in healthy ways. Take radical responsibility for your own triggers and for helping your husband's triggers.

This is why boyfriend and girlfriend relationships are so dangerous. In those situations, we choose partners that trigger us immensely but they never stick around long enough to help heal us. Our triggers may actually scare them off! Thus, perpetuating the wound and reinforcing our lack of self-worth and trust in love, actually causing more damage and pain in the long run. Save the inner work for your husband. Choose someone who is also committed to growth and healing. Remember that our childhood traumas are relational wounds, and therefore require relational healing.

During this time, regardless of whether both of you are working or not, learn to live on only his income. Factor only your husband's income on important life decisions such as where to live, what house to buy, and what kind of a lifestyle to have. Remembering that this is only a season of life. You get to have it all in other seasons of life. If you are working, put away your money in savings and investments for the next era so you can stay home with your babies. If you choose wisely, your husband should be able to provide for you and your babies, as long as you guys don't overextend your lifestyle in this phase of life. In my first book, I talked about prioritizing staying home with my babies and keeping a minimalist lifestyle and I have zero regrets! I didn't have the lifestyle that I have now but my babies are healthy and that was the number one priority. I had a successful real estate business in my twenties but gave it up to become a stay-at-home wife and mom after marrying Irfan. Best decision I ever made!

Baby-Making and Mothering Era: I don't recommend waiting too long to have your babies. Ideally you should have your babies in your twenties or at the latest early 30s. Granted of course that you are healthy enough to do so. The truth is that if you are reading this book and doing your inner work, you are already in the top 1% of homo sapien health. The western world has lost its marbles. We have made child rearing and relationships in general so scary and complicated that humans may be on their way of becoming an endangered species. Human fertility has been rapidly declining and many people are also afraid of having children.

The truth is that we were designed to have children. They keep us sane, balanced, and focused on the right values in life. Motherhood is your birthright and you are fully capable of having a beautiful motherhood experience. In the first three years of a child's life, it is essential that they spend time with their mother at home. This lack of essential bonding period between mother and child is the reason that so many humans currently need inner work. This interruption in maternal bonding in the first three years of life is the reason for this intense human craving for connection and yet inability to metabolize love. Do whatever you need to do to give this gift to your babies and to yourself.

Your assignment in this era: Have your babies in your twenties and then spend the first three years of their life with them. I promise there will be plenty of time for creating your career and wealth later on. Don't rob yourself and your babies of this essential time. Your children will not need inner work if you give them your nurturing attention, love, and guidance in the first three years of life. The rest of your parenting journey will be so much easier as well. Children who have received this time to bond with a physically and emotionally present mother are very easy to raise compared to those that have not. I used this era to nurture my babies and also spend time reading, learning, doing more inner work which ended up helping in creating my Wealthy Woman Era!

Allow mothering and parenting to be fun. I have so much fun with my kids and don't subscribe to the motherhood misery narrative at all. One of the most important gifts you can give your children is your romantic marriage. Make sure you spend time every evening pouring into your partner's cup. Motherhood shouldn't rob you of your pleasure, femininity, and playfulness. My union is my most important embodiment and gift to my kids and I want them to learn that marriage is sexy and fun!

Wealthy Woman Era: As your children get older and become a little more self-sufficient, you will have more time and a new kind of energy. This is the time to start and create something of your own. My wealthy woman era started in 2017. My husband was providing a beautiful lifestyle for us, but I wanted to use my gifts and create something of my own. I think modern women desire to have this wealthy woman season but often end up creating this at the expense of everything else. I believe this feminine blueprint is the reason I activated so much wealth and abundance in my life.

If I had tried and forced this stage earlier in my life, it would have been laden with guilt, hustling, and juggling. When you are trying to do everything at once, you often fail or half ass at everything. Because I took my time nurturing myself, my marriage, and my children, I was able to activate my wealthy woman era from overflow. I used all the skills, education, and embodiment I had acquired up until this point to create healing for others while creating wealth and legacy.

Your assignment in this era: As your children start school, use this time wisely to start planning your next season of life. Who do you want to be in this season? What do you want to create? Would you need to go back to school to start a career? Perhaps you want to launch a small business for yourself. You have the rest of your life to live out your wealthy woman era from a place of fullness and radiance. I will talk more about this era in a future chapter. We really do get to have it all, but not just all at once.

Creating Your Own Feminine Blueprint

So, what if you are reading this at an age where it feels like you "missed the boat" so to speak? I believe we all get to win no matter what cards we are dealt. Some people are lucky to discover this work early on and be able to perfectly follow the ideal blueprint, others are dealt a different hand at life. I believe we all have the ability to bloom where we are planted. Get crystalline clear of your true heart's desires. What do you really want? If everything was available and an easy option, then what would you choose? Once you have some clarity of what you truly desire, drop in at the desired blueprint stage and make it a priority. So, if you are in your late 30s and really desire marriage and babies, then really prioritize that. Stop putting finding a partner on the back burner and focusing on your career.

When I shared this timeline with my students and YouTube audience, even the women who were initially triggered thanked me later. Many women were currently putting off motherhood for no good reason. Prioritizing things that have no biological or other timeline over something that clearly does! I have received hundreds of emails and private messages from women in their 30s saying they decided not to put off something so important to them and get going while they still have time.

I believe the blueprint I shared above can be customized to meet you wherever you are in your journey. It should help you see your life in seasons which I believe is a very useful way for women to have it all in a feminine way that honors the way we were created.

Journal Prompts:

What feminine season of life am I in? What do I need to prioritize in this season?

____

____

____

What needs to be removed from my life currently to truly focus on the most important things?

____

____

____

Do I need to create a customized blucprint for my life? What will that look like?

____

____

____

CHAPTER *Six*
WOMEN ARE THE GATEKEEPERS OF DNA

Men are like Waffles, Women are like Spaghetti is a book by authors Pam and Bill Ferrel which perfectly describes how men and women process life differently. Men tend to process life in compartments. Moving from one "box" to the next, with most boxes never touching each other. For women, life is intertwined like spaghetti. Our relationships impact our work, our work impacts our friendships, and so on. Female success is generally perceived differently than male success. A man can be very successful in his career and that is enough. For women, success is a combination of health, relationships, parenting, friendships, how we feel in our bodies, and so much more.

When a woman tries to find success the male way, by only focusing on her career, she at some point in life finds herself empty and lost. I have had the pleasure of coaching some of the most powerful women on the planet, and can confidently attest that women view and judge standards of success differently than men. Women who over-optimize their masculine success and become overly successful in just one area still feel like something is massively missing from their lives. They do not feel successful. I had fallen into that trap as well having had success in my real estate career in my twenties. Even though everyone around me was impressed with what I had created at such a young age, I felt empty inside. I did not feel successful.

I teach women to upgrade and live well in all areas of importance and priority in their lives, not just career and money. Self-Aware Barbies have a habit of over optimizing just one or two areas of their lives at the expense of everything else. For a woman to feel full and fulfilled, she needs to be overflowing in all of her desires. We really do get to have it all as long as we can clearly define what "having it all" means to us as individuals. As women, we can't talk about success without talking about all the important areas of our life, especially relationships. Men and relationships in general can either become a huge distraction to your success or a huge asset. This is one area where women must learn to choose wisely.

My first memory as a child (around five years old) was one of being sexually molested by a male babysitter. Trauma has a way of making a home in your body and subconscious mind. Running a parasitic virus behind the scenes while you go about your everyday life. I spent most of my life feeling scared, ashamed, and stuck in my wounded masculine energy as a result of that and other traumatic experiences all throughout my childhood. I was stuck in phase 2 of the Self-Aware Barbie. I was a slave to my to-do lists and constant need to keep moving. Never allowing myself a moment of time and space to heal. It was like I had all this LOVE and LIGHT to share with the world but it was coming through as a tiny pinhole behind all the pain and fear. But as God always does when we ask and allow, I was shown the way to cure my heart.

It was not through hiding and fearing. But through going towards fear and pain and truly healing it once and for all. Healing the Masculine Wounds of my heart. Healing the Feminine Wounds of my soul. As part of my healing, I had to integrate more of my goddess and savage energy. Especially when it came to my relationships. Goddess energy is when our human part is in communication with our divine part. The two work together in a beautiful synergy I like to call divine union. Boundaries are created in this realm of goddess energy. Most people try to create boundaries in the physical plane and fail. More on boundaries in a later chapter.

Savage is the understanding and honoring of our DNA and bloodlines. It goes so much deeper than goddess energy. Goddess is your right. Savage is your divine duty. This is when a woman takes her rightful place as a gatekeeper and protector of DNA. Savage isn't just about becoming a mother. It's an amplifier of energy, just like alcohol and money. When predators amplify savage energy, there is pain, suffering, destruction for all of us. When kind-hearted, loving people amplify this energy, everyone feels loved and held. Predators already know how to be savage. They were never conditioned out of this energy in the first place. It's all the kind hearted, healthy people who have forgotten! And this creates a huge problem for all of us. We can't let predators win the survival of the fittest race.

Genuine, kind-hearted, loving people must become just as dangerous to predators as they are to us and our children. Power must be matched with power. Savage is not only your birthright but also your service to humanity. People-pleasing, over-giving, and over-doing makes you and your loved ones an open target to manipulators and users. It makes you and your family look weak. Who are you trying to impress anyway? Who are you trying to be kind to so you can get some fake validation and applause? In interviews with convicted predators, the one common trend for the victims they choose was a weak family unit. They go after the low hanging fruit. I was the low hanging fruit with parents trying to earn everyone's approval and validation. I can't help but imagine how different my childhood could have been if I had a strong family unit. A mother and father that predators thought twice before coming near. Although I have no regrets or resentments towards anyone, especially not my parents, I can say confidently that if they had invested even 25% of the energy they invested into other people into their own family and home, I wouldn't have had to deal with the abuse that I did. The predators that targeted me knew that I had a weak backbone from my weak family unit. My parents were too kind, too generous, and they were no match for predators.

I read somewhere decades ago that most childhood sexual abuse happens with people the child knows and often someone well liked and trusted by the parents. This was true in my case as well, so I trust no one when it comes to my children. This is a decision I made a long time ago. Seeing everyone as a potential predator when it comes to my children has helped me keep my eyes and ears open and my savage energy activated. **Read this twice: Moms and dads should be dangerous to predators. Let them see us and run in the other direction. Let them cross the street so they don't have to pass by us late at night. Let them shiver and stay up at night worried about what we could do to them if they cross our paths.**

My mission is to raise and uplift the family unit by helping women do their inner work. We all rise when women are restored as the gatekeepers of DNA. As a woman, you seal your child's future before you are even in a relationship. Before you lay down with a man, you have already decided your unborn child's future. Even if that union does not result in a child, the trauma that you will carry from having predator partners will impact any future children in the womb. You are the most important gate and decision point in the bloodline. Females of all species have chosen mates very intentionally and carefully until recently when the homo sapien female has decided to ditch any and all mating standards. Even the birds and reptiles give more thought and care with whom they lay with.

Women must raise their standards by becoming the savage and gatekeeping DNA. Savage is the understanding and honoring of our DNA and bloodlines. Being shuffled between the eastern and western cultures in my childhood had immense benefits that I didn't quite understand at the time. It was interesting to see how much eastern culture valued DNA and bloodlines. This wasn't honored as much in my western life. After studying religion, spirituality, evolution, and anthropology, predators, and providers, I now see the value in concerning yourself with DNA and bloodlines.

For most of human history, the providers/protectors and good-hearted humans have outnumbered the predators. The way it was supposed to be. The elders in the tribes made sure only a certain type of genome made into the future. Men who provided and protected and took care of their families got married and had children. These were the original Alpha males. This is now rapidly changing all over the world.

Men had to jump through hoops to prepare themselves as the leaders of their family and society. No providing, no family, no sex. It was pretty easy. With the promotion of free sex in the western world, this has changed. Any man can pretty much sleep with a rainbow of women at a moment's notice. The men getting the highest amounts of free sex are predatory in nature. **The way things are going in the western dating world, the predators will soon outnumber the providers.** And that is not a world I want to leave behind for my children and future descendants. Until very recently, men had to jump through hoops getting an excellent education, making a successful career, impressing a woman›s family, and then asking her hand in marriage to be able to have a family. Now a man can pick up a woman at a bar and make a baby with her, over a freaking drink! Does this sound like great DNA to be sending into our species' future?

When women were the gatekeepers of DNA, a man had to prove his worth and providing and protecting capabilities to have children. Those were the standards and so men lived up to it. Now that men have access to sex without any prerequisites, more predatory DNA will make it into the future. These men are the ones likely to sleep with as many women as possible. Some of these encounters will result in children. Leaving the woman to raise them alone.

In these situations, not only do we have a non-provider/protector DNA, we also have the added conditioning of being raised without a present father. Not to mention the mother line womb wounds that result from a woman devaluing herself in this way. Your body is not a repository for dirty DNA. It is unnatural for good hearted, kind people to abandon their children. And abandonment starts when you lay down with someone without commitment.

DNA has consequences. I get it, babies are cute and it's strange to think of them as coming from predator DNA. But those babies grow up to become lost, broken adults. When women stop gatekeeping, we all face the consequences. There is a lot we still don't understand about DNA. Science is a relatively new field. But as fast as ancient knowledge is becoming scientifically verified, we should be all concerned. More of what we thought was outdated truths of a generation long gone, is now becoming scientific fact.

Girlfriend is not a Status

There are cons and pros to every culture, and while I don't agree with a lot of things from my culture, one thing that I really admire from the Pakistani culture is their deep understanding and innate knowledge of relationships. Pakistani people have one of the highest relationship success rates I have ever seen. Unfortunately, because of my less than ideal childhood, I grew up mostly resenting my culture and threw out the baby with the bathwater. It was only after I started studying evolution, psychology and all the major religions of the world that I realized how lucky I was to have been born Pakistani-American. Today, I am able to use both science and eastern culture as examples in my work.

In Pakistani culture, there is no concept of boyfriend and girlfriend. Of course, children born to Pakistani immigrants and living in the west sometimes get themselves into these imaginary roles. I got curious about this no girlfriend/boyfriend thing and realized that this was a completely made up status and problematic to both men and women. It is not honored in any religion and also not a legal status. In my culture, they understand that men and women are very different and honor their natural ways of being in relationships. They avoid a lot of emotional and physical turmoil by not engaging in boyfriend and girlfriend relationships.

These imaginary relationships cause emotional and financial damage in a lot of women's lives. You shouldn't be held back in life due to these imaginary relationships. The female nervous system and hormones conceive these imaginary relationships as very much real. While the male nervous system of predatory men takes them as no big deal. We have this concept in the eastern world that has served me well. It loosely translates into "foreign male energy." Anyone that is not a blood relative like your father, brother, and son, is considered foreign male energy. We do not spend time in private with anyone that is foreign male energy. This keeps people with bad intentions away from you and people with good intentions respecting you and seeing you as the ultimate Goddess. Until a man claims you in a legal and spiritual marriage, he is foreign energy and has no right to be with you.

Stop laying down with men who haven't legally, spiritually, emotionally, and financially claimed you. Resume your reign as the genetic gatekeeper. Providing for his family is a sign of emotional, spiritual, and physical well-being in a man. It has little to do with money and everything to do with DNA. Stop letting men off the hook by laying down with predators. Or going 50/50 with neither here nor there men, and getting into imaginary relationships with the girlfriend trap. Girlfriend is not a status. It's not a legal, emotional, or religious status. There is no such thing as a man test driving a woman before choosing her for marriage. This is a huge scam and women are happily co-signing it.

These are the kind of decisions a woman must make once and uphold with every man. Unfortunately, many women have these guidelines with men they don't like and then once someone they find cute comes along, all their personal values go out the door.

No one should get to test drive you for years while deciding if you are the one or not. Here is a news flash: Healthy men know right away if you are the one or not. The ones that need to date you for years, become your boyfriend, and shack up with you to decide are not healthy men. And you are not in your right mind to allow this type of behavior in your life. I'm always shocked to see women flaunting their boyfriends on social media and in real life as if they have won some kind of Nobel Peace Prize!

Love Lists and Rotational Dating

You may be wondering how the hell are you supposed to date when you are not to be alone with foreign male energy. Let's first take a moment to define what dating is. Dating is courting for marriage. It involves going to lunch, dinner, and other outdoor activities with the sole purpose of getting to see if someone is a good match for marriage. Dating is not going to Netflix and chill with someone in the bedroom. It's not about him showing up to your place at odd hours of the night. Both of these scenarios serve predatory men and devalue the hell out of you.

Rotational dating is a concept from the Eastern world that has been modernized and brought into the Western world. You court several men at the same time, becoming no man's girlfriend, until you accept someone's proposal. Simple as that. I have taught tens of thousands of women of all ages and all cultures this concept and have thousands of success stories. And those are just the ones that women have taken the time to inform me about.

Some women think that they are doing something wrong if they date this way. They don't understand what we mean by dating here, then I can see why they would misunderstand the concept. Dating does not mean sleeping with men. Sex should be reserved for marriage (more on this in a later section). Dating should not offer commitment or wife benefits until he proposes, you accept, and there is a legal and spiritual ceremony in front of at least a handful of witnesses. A society of healthy people holds both men and women accountable for their actions in relationships. Relationships should not be created in secrecy. Without the witness of other people of your union, there is no accountability for men to respect, honor, protect, and provide for you. Your union affects not only you, but the whole planet and the destiny of humanity.

The first step in rotational dating is creating a love list. A love list is a list of personal values and qualities that you are looking for in your future husband. It also serves as a vision board! This is the first step I started with. Write down the qualities you want him to have that match your personal values. Next to each quality write down how you need to be a reciprocal of those qualities to be a vibrational match to him. Because remember that he will also have some qualities he is looking for in his future wife. So, for example, if you wrote down "masculine" then you must be the reciprocal quality "feminine" to be his match.

The next step is to categorize your love list into three parts. Non-negotiables (Basic Requirements), Satisfiers (Differentiators), Delighters (Oh, wow! I get to have this too!).

Non-negotiables will generally not make you excited if you get them, because these are things that are expected. For example, you won't be too excited if he isn't a serial killer because that is expected! With Satisfiers you will be happy if you get them and very unhappy if you don't. These are the main differentiators between this guy or that one. Delighters are things that are not deal breakers for you but you're not mad about these bonuses either. Some men will delight you in the dating period and make you forget your non-negotiables!! Remember that these types of delighters are not always sustainable in long term marriage. So, make sure not to be dazzled out of your first two categories.

Sheena used to say that boyfriends will always excite women more than husbands. A boyfriend comes to have fun with you with very little concern for your long-term well-being. He will be long gone from your life so why concern himself with your future. A husband is "boring" because he wants to buy you a house, worries about providing health insurance, and is stressed about saving for retirement. Go for the long-term intention of a man, marriage is a long game! You are in it forever.

Something else to beware of: As we have already established, the Divine Feminine heart is a bottomless pit of desires and there is absolutely nothing wrong with that! Something worth noting here is that as expectations and trends change in marriage, sometimes we can start treating delighters as our satisfiers or non-negotiables. Of course, your divine union gets to keep growing and evolving, but never from a place of annoyance or dissatisfaction. So, for example, let's say you have found the one and are happily married. Then you met a couple that is overly lovey dovey in public with grand shows of PDA. Although you have a very romantic marriage, your partner is not big on PDA. His point is to keep romance sacred and between the two of you. Suddenly, you start feeling like your husband is "broken," or otherwise lacking something. You have now not only started taking all the non-negotiables and satisfiers for granted, but are passive aggressively punishing him over a delighter!!

The correct way to handle this situation is from a place of adventure and curiosity. You can go to him and say, "*Wow, I love how our new friends are fearless about their love for each other. Wouldn't it be nice to try this out as well.*" This way you are growing and trying something new together versus making him feel unappreciated for everything else he does bring to the table.

When I was rotational dating in 2008, I was dating several men (most of whom my mom or best friend at the time had introduced me to). We spoke on the phone briefly, went to dinner to get to know each other's values and interests. All the men were also rotational dating for marriage. One of the men in my rotation asked me to be his girlfriend, and I politely declined. He said he was serious about getting married and wanted to get to know me and my son better. I will share the exact script I used below.

No Girlfriend Script

"Awww, I'm so flattered! I love spending time with you too. But as you know I am looking for marriage. I have decided to only

accept marriage proposals at this time. I will only be committing to my husband."

Sidenote: He did propose a few days later, but he wasn't a good match for my love list. He wanted the jet set lifestyle and I wanted to settle into a quiet, comfy life at home. Shortly after, I decided to sign up for an online marriage matchmaking site for Indian, Pakistani, and Middle Eastern people. Within the same day, I met my now husband, Irfan, and my picture hadn't even been approved yet! He lived in a different state than me but Irfan was a consultant at the time and traveled for a living. He was scheduled to come to Chicago in two weeks. We decided to talk on the phone for those two weeks and then go to dinner once he was in town. He was also looking for marriage and rotational dating at the time.

We hit it off immediately, he had all of the qualities from my love list. We went to dinner a few times. He met my friends, son, and family, and he proposed in two weeks. I accepted the proposal. We were married in two months. The day I accepted the proposal was when I messaged the other people on my rotation and let them know I was now engaged. Irfan did the same that day. I love my culture's approach to drama free dating and engagements. This is why I teach women from all cultures this approach in the current crazy dating scene. When people hear my story, they think everyone has to get married fast when rotational dating. This is NOT true! You can take as much time as you need dating or even being engaged. This is just how it worked out for me.

Sheena had been diagnosed with cancer earlier that year and wanted nothing more than to see me married. She told me it was her last wish. This is why my timeline was so fast. Rotational dating will have men chasing to get you off the dating market. Their animalistic human Alpha male energy kicks in when they like you and can smell foreign male energy on your person from your other dates. However, when my clients are rushing to accept proposals, even I am a little skeptical. It's okay to slow down the process and take your time.

Life Force and Why Sex before Marriage is Dangerous for You

Your most important asset is your life force energy, especially as a woman. Your feminine life force is the raw manifestation energy that you can cash in for the life of your wildest desires. This energy can be used to create life, abundance, health, beauty, and pretty much anything else you desire. When you lay down with men before marriage, they steal your potent life force energy. With no investment made in claiming you, providing, and protecting for you, it's an energetic rape that you co-sign.

They can now use that energy to build themselves up. More confidence, better health, more money, promotions, opportunities, and more women are just some of the benefits your life force gives them. Have you noticed that the more women a man sleeps with, the more confident he becomes, and the more women seem to want him? He does that by taking your life force and using it for his personal gain and benefit.

He becomes better by taking your life force while you lower your value, opening yourself up for pregnancy, healthy issues, emotional damage, sexual trauma, and the fact that his sperm alters your DNA.

I honor each woman's choice. But choice should come with knowing the consequences. Then it's an educated choice. You have the choice of using your life force for your own benefit. Creating a beautiful life experience. Money, health, more beauty. All of that and more is an alternative to giving your energy away to others. Use it for yourself and share your Lakshmi energy with your future husband and children. No need to give it away to men who don't care about your well-being.

Years ago, a friend of mine decided to start sleeping with a man she had recently met. He was leading her on about a possible future marriage and she felt pressured to sleep with him. Immediately after she started having UTIs and other female health issues. She didn't have health insurance and couldn't afford all these visits to the doctor and the medications that she now suddenly needed. She was also on the verge of losing her job since this new man would show up to have sex with her anytime he wished. When she confided in me what was going on, I had her call him to ask for health insurance and money for medical care. He got so upset and said she was trying to use him for money. Of course, I knew he wouldn't agree to providing even a dime for her. Why would he? She was not his wife. Why should he concern himself with her health? This was such a wakeup call for her and she finally understood why my culture was so strict about sex before marriage. It is to protect women not oppress them!

Having multiple sexual partners increases your emotional health issues, medical issues, hormonal issues, ages you faster, wastes your time, and so much more. We have not evolved to have the number of sexual partners people these days have. I used to believe this was common knowledge. That every woman had been taught the hormonal dangers of laying down with a man before marriage. The truth is, a man can sleep with a woman and feel rejuvenated, uplifted, or nothing at all. For a woman, there are dire consequences. Evolution created us to be the gatekeepers of DNA. So, by the time you actually slept with a man, the assumption was that you have done your research on his providing/protecting and DNA. And because you found him worthy enough to sleep with him, nature now intoxicated you with a hormone fueled filter. Because a child could result from this union, it made sense for nature to now block out all his flaws. Keeping you together for the child's sake. Sleeping with a man not only blinds you to his shortcomings, and often down right predatory behavior, but his sperm also alters your DNA. This and more is why the ancients took marriage and sex so seriously.

I have so many more horror stories I can share with you about the dangers of giving men sexual access before marriage, allow me to share one more. I was a part of a Facebook group years ago on dating and relationships. A woman posted: (I am paraphrasing based on memory):

"Every man I sleep with tries to choke me during sex. It really hurts. What should I do?"

I could not believe the responses from the other women in the group. Truly an example of the blind leading the blind. People were advising her to sit these men down and have conversations about her needs and boundaries. There were comments on "safe words" and other signals of distress during sex. Are you kidding me? Not one person told her to immediately stop having sex with strangers. I think I probably came across as almost sarcastic when I posted "*Why are you having sex with strange men? Immediately stop having sex.*" Her immediate reply suggested she didn't realize this was an option! I am not sure what kind of weird matrix we are living in where it is news to women that they can say no to sex.

Even with the scientific evidence we now have, we continue to turn a blind eye to what's happening to our bodies, minds, and souls. Not to mention the sheer danger of sleeping with a stranger who can literally choke us to death with his bare hands. Value yourself. Raise your standards. Get intentional about what it takes for a man to have access to your most prized asset. In my personal and educated opinion, a man should be willing and able to provide at least the following evolutionary basics to have you in marriage.

Masculine Containment

The divine masculine containment around you and the relationship includes way more than just money. It is the literal "band around the house" from which the word husband is derived from. His commitment, accountability, and ownership of the relationship is a huge part of what he provides. Here is a quick breakdown of what the masculine provides in relationships.

Psychological Protection. The structure and energetics of a lifelong commitment to you. That he will be there for you through the thick and thin of life. The ups and downs, the good times and the bad times. He should be interested in your family and getting to know them and form a tribal bond between his family and yours. This is something you need to be able and willing to receive. I have seen many women reject this energy from their husband because of previous bad experiences with men or their father.

Physical Protection. This is the hero energy that most men spend their entire lives wanting to be respected and acknowledged for. He stands up for you in private and public. He wants the best for you even at times when you may be in disagreement.

Shelter/Housing. He should be able to provide a place of residence for you and any future children. This doesn›t have to be a mansion but it should feel safe. Remember that you will have many homes throughout your long union, God willing.

Food. Going back to our hunter/gatherer programming, healthy men pride themselves in being able to feed their families.

Common Utilities. Electricity, water, gas, phone. This should be connected to providing shelter and the basics that come with that.

Medical Insurance and Costs (your medical needs go up when you are sexually active).

Clothing. This doesn't have to be designer wear, but again goes under providing shelter for you.

Children's Needs. You should have the option to stay home with your children and raise them.

Transportation. Basic transportation.

Here are the answers to some common questions that come up:

Q. What if he is unable to provide? Should we leave men behind who can't provide? Don't they deserve to have a family?

A. You are not a charity and neither is your womb. Being able to provide for his family is a sign of basic male health and readiness for marriage.

Q. Why should he pay for these things if I already make so much money?

A. Because providing isn't about money. It's about his rights as a man and your rights as a woman. It's also about emotional and physical health and well-being. A man who can provide is ready to be a husband and a father. He has been training and grooming himself to be in that position pretty much all his life. In his own eyes and the eyes of society, he has now earned the "man" title.

If you are a high achieving, high income woman, it's even more important that you let him provide for you. This will create instant polarity in your marriage and protect you from predatory men wanting to take advantage of you.

Q. What's wrong with 50/50?

A. Men don't do transactions with women they love. They have transactions with co-workers, friends, and placeholders. Mainly so they can save their money and then finally provide for their dream woman when she shows up.

By going 50/50, you are actually preventing a man from growing in love with you. Take your 50% and invest it in your own future. Invest in high income skill sets, building up your portfolio, and upgrading your lifestyle. In my opinion, a good solid financial future also includes having high standards and healthy boundaries in relationships. You shouldn't have to pay a grown man's bills. I'm embarrassed for him as I even type this.

What king would allow a woman to pay half his bills! So embarrassing for both of you.

Cord Cutting Exercise to Restore Your Life Force Energy Lost through Sexual Encounters

This is my cord cutting invocation. Invocations are 21-day rituals that we perform with the aid of our guides, angels, and God. This ritual can help us to restore our energy after encounters with difficult or toxic people. It can also help break generational curses, or sexual entanglements. Please note that this ritual does not replace the therapy most women need after having sexual encounters with men before marriage.

Recite this for 21 days. If you miss a day, start the 21 days count again. I personally love to light a candle and call upon my guides and angels to assist me before I start reciting this. It really helps to recite this daily at about the same time. Within an hour of the same time is okay.

Dear Divine (God, Universe, Source, Higher Self),

I call upon my loving ancestors, my personal guides, Angels, and God to assist me in this cord cutting ritual.

Dear Divine, I am now released of any ties, cords, entanglements, soul contracts, and vows that no longer serve me.

Dear Divine, I now return back to sender what is not mine.

I now call back all and any missing parts of myself back home.

Please restore my energy to its original soul blueprint as intended at my soul's origination.

Dear Divine, I am now healed and whole in all directions of time and space.

Please cleanse my energy and restore every cell in my body with your golden divine light.

I am now cleansed and renewed with golden divine light.

And so it is!

Divine Union

"*But what if my needs change later and I would have agreed to this now?*" My client asked over the phone on our weekly coaching session.

"*Then you will go to your husband and let him know that your needs have changed and have a discussion about it like grown ups do." I replied back.*

"*Oh, I can do that,*" she almost whispered back. The client I was speaking to was a high level executive of a huge Fortune 500 company. This woman had the kind of aura and personality that would intimidate even the most confident among us. She had risen from rags to riches and had created a beautiful life for herself and her family. She had apparently missed the memo, like most of us, on marriage and what we get to have, be, and do.

I continued explaining to her, *"Babe, your union is a living, breathing, evolving document. You and your husband are allowed to change your minds and modify things at any point. In fact, the most successful marriages are between two growth mindset people."* I could literally feel the sign of relief and paradigm shift on the other line. I paused to see if she wanted to add something and then continued. *"Marriage is for the long haul. If you do this right, you will be married for 50-80 years depending on your age and life span. Not only will you change your mind many times throughout this timeframe, you both will be completely different people as you go through the various seasons of life."*

Fixed mindset people have given marriage a really tough reputation! These are the people who blame each other's perceived "written in stone" personality traits for their marital problems. When you see someone as a fixed stage and incapable to learn, grow, and evolve, there is only one way to go from there, and that's to divorce court. I believe more than 97% of marriages can be saved, granted they are healthy enough to be in a legally binding contract like marriage, have similar values, and a growth mindset. That is the formula right there. We attract the person that has the most capacity to heal us. Everything in nature strives towards more life. Nature wants to expand and heal. It is natural for us to want to grow, change, and evolve with our partners.

In my opinion, the most important thing we should be looking for in a partner is a growth mindset and similar values. Some people mistake values for interests and hobbies. It's okay to have a difference in interests and hobbies, but values should be similar. I want to share an example from my rotational dating journey to highlight the difference between interests and values. One of the men on my rotation was a successful attorney who shared custody of his son with his ex-wife. He was well-spoken, kind, and shared some mutual friends with me. He simply "made sense" to my family and friends who thought we would be a great match. On our third dinner date, as he was driving me back home, he said something that made me go home and clarify my love list.

"*You need someone who will stay home with you and your son and create a nice comfortable, family life,*" he said. "*I am looking for someone I can take to nightclubs, host parties with, and travel the world. I really like you, but noticed you declined my invitation to go dancing and party after dinner on all three occasions. That's the lifestyle I envision for me and my future wife.*"

That right there was a huge difference in our personal values. I'm so glad he was honest enough to catch it and say it! He shared that he was engaged a year ago and his fiancée had broken off the engagement because she couldn't get him to stop going to nightclubs. That's what he really valued in life. He had gotten married and had his son young in life and wanted to be wild and free now that he had the chance. As we discussed in chapter four, personal values are important guidelines for how we live and process life.

Having this huge difference in personal values would have been a disaster. I modified my love list with his useful insight and got even more clear on the kind of relationship and home environment I wanted to have.

Yesterday was the 15-year anniversary of when my husband and I first met. During our union, Irfan and I have grown and changed in so many ways. The one thing that has remained consistent and constant throughout our union is our personal values. Our similar values make our union robust. They are the foundations on which the entire relationship is created. Being on the same page in life on all the big things makes everything else so much easier. Similar values make it easier to parent your children as well.

Our values for marriage and family are a combination of the honoring of our evolutionary history, our cultural roles, and the divine feminine and masculine desires. This is the foundation or the cake of our marriage. The frosting and sprinkles on top are the modern twists and flavors we have added to this blueprint. I chose a man who has the same values as me when it comes to marriage, family, children, and our individual and collective roles. With the larger things decided, we have spent our time working on what we consider the "small kinks" and have meta updated each other over the years. Meta-updating is the process of two people who respect and trust each other's authority, end up inching closer and closer to each other's beliefs and viewpoints over time.

Shortly after we got married, both of our inner wounds started surfacing up wanting to be healed in the safety of our relationship. This is when most couples start fearing that they may have chosen the wrong partner. The right partner will trigger the hell out of your childhood wounds and vice versa, so you can finally heal. They seem like the problem but they are actually the solution. Marriage is the closest thing we have to recreating the dynamics of our birth family. This is why marriage is so triggering! It reminds us too closely of all the stuff we must work through. Because of our similar values, we didn't jump ship. We stayed the course and helped each other heal. We provided a safe space for things to come up and for us to sooth each other. We created new narratives, new stories, and new core beliefs on what we both get to have in love, life, and relationship. If having healthy, vibrant, robust relationships is the ultimate sign of healing, then I am happy to report that we have healed.

Irfan and I have made each other our #1 priority–yes, even before our children. We prioritize our marriage before work, extended family, friends, and even our own children. This actually serves not only our kids but has become a healing force for our entire extended family, community, and following on social media. We repeatedly get messages from people saying our union and family is the first healthy example they have seen. By not making it about other people, and making each other the center of the universe, we ended up helping more people than we can even conceive. By allowing our union to be a safe place for the both of us first, it became a safe place for our children, extended families, and dare I say, even the planet.

Here are some concepts that have helped us along the way, many of which I teach in my online courses.

Marital Values. Decide early on what kind of a union, marriage, and home life you want to have. We decided we are both very traditional and love the masculine and feminine polarities which match our evolutionary history. This way we are not fighting an uphill battle against our DNA, hormones, and nervous systems. Life becomes unnecessarily hard when you try to go against the construction of your natural makeup.

Marital Commandments. Create a set of "commandments" for your marriage when things are good. This will serve as guidelines when one or both of you are triggered. One of our commandments is that we will never doubt each other's intentions. This has helped so much when my abandonment wounds would get triggered early on in our marriage. Learning how to not immediately jump into attacking my husband's intentions was a completely new skill set for me. I had to learn to ask him questions about why he said or did something while assuming good will. What a powerful skill set to have in your communication tool box!

Couple Grid. Your couple grid is an imaginary, albeit, potent energetic bubble around your union. Imagine you and your husband as the center of a bubble. You must learn to honor and respect your union from inside this bubble. Decisions are made together, as a joined unit, disagreements must be sorted out, household rules must be created, etc. This puts your unit as the center of your life and gives the world a powerful message about the strength of your marriage. Your careers, your children, your friends, everyone else gets to benefit from the robust love of your relationship grid.

Family Unit/Household Grid. After the couple grid, I want you to envision a second grid, this one encompasses your entire home and family unit. This energetic grid places your family unit as the center of your world. It creates the structure and holds the flow of love. This doesn't mean you "keep people out" but instead you keep love close and front and center.

Inner Work. Be open and willing to do the inner work together. Learn each other's triggers, and decide to soothe them to make each other and your entire union healthier and more robust over time.

Lesson: Choose a man based on your personal values and who is ready, willing, and capable of providing and protecting. This honors his DNA as well as yours. Create a couple grid and a safe place to heal and become the relationship of your dreams.

Journal Prompts:

What feminine lessons did I learn from my earliest caregivers about relationships?

What masculine lessons did I learn from my earliest caregivers about relationships?

What are my new core beliefs around what I get to have in relationships?

What are my new personal values around relationships?

____

____

____

What does a man need to provide to have access to me energetically, emotionally, and sexually?

____

____

____

Parenting, the Easy Way

One of the deepest regrets of my life is not being very present in my oldest son's life for the first few years. I was going through a divorce while pregnant with him and suddenly thrust into extreme survival mode when he was born. Running a successful real estate business, while being a student at Northwestern University, I missed the precious first few years of the bonding that occurs between a mother and a child. I was blessed that my parents and siblings picked up the slack and he always had a safe place with them, however, that is time I will never get back. Armaan was four when I married Irfan. Being able to give him a healthy, robust, masculine father is one of my most winning moments in life. I knew that if I had any more children, I would want to be home to raise them myself.

I know daycares are very touchy subjects and many prominent figures have been canceled for presenting the shocking data of what they do to children's psyches. Shocked to uncover this, I became curious as to why anyone would care if some people presented uncomfortable stats about daycares? Turns out, daycares were created as a last resort. They were only to be used in extreme situations by single parents who had no access to any other relative for help. They were never meant to be used the way they are used now as a casual option.

Babies need to attach and bond with consistent caregivers, ideally the one whose womb they came out of, for at least the first three years of life. This allows them to trust that the world is a safe and loving place and the people who love them are trustworthy. This is simply not present in daycare environments where there is a revolving door of come and go employees who simply change your diaper and feed you. This interrupts a very delicate and important process in the human psyche.

So why was this information attacked? Why are so many researchers terrified about speaking up against daycares? Turns out it's for the same reason that marriage and motherhood is under attack. This connection really sunk in for me when I recently heard a character in a Pakistani TV serial say the following line:

"How can Pakistan be successful as a nation when nearly half the country (the females) don't work and are provided for?"

My heart nearly jumped out of my body when I heard this. Of course, I want women in Pakistan to work outside the home if they choose, however, that bit about the country *needing them* to work hit a cord! Only a few short weeks later, I discovered Suzanne Venkar's YouTube channel talking about this exact thing!! Corporations thrive on the educated, cheap labor that women bring to the table. Keeping women single and childless benefits the labor force. With no family ties or sick children keeping women from needing time off, you have access to cheap labor willing and able to invest all their time and energy in their jobs. For the ones that do have families, we have daycares. They sell them to us casually and even try to convince us of the whole myth of babies needing to be socialized.

We are certainly not perfect as parents; however, I feel very confident in the parenting strategies we have used. Our 19-year-old son is always complimenting our parenting, so I will take that as a huge success. Just like our union, we have heavily relied on evolution and our traditional culture to form the foundation of our parenting style. We didn't want a household where children were punished or disciplined, so we adopted the "natural consequences" technique and it has been a game changer! When our children make a mistake, we let the mistake be the "discipline." It turns out the world offers its own set of "punishments" and parents don't really have to step in and discipline the children on top of that. For example, if a child oversleeps on a school day, instead of screaming, yelling, or taking things away, let "being late for school and getting a tardy" be the natural consequence. This will teach him or her to better manage their time or face the normal and real consequences that occur in life without turning you into a dictator. These concepts can be hard to learn and embody at first, but once it clicks in, it's life changing. Keeping a calm, loving, and fun household environment is very important to us.

Our biggest parenting strategy has been to give our children the best feminine and masculine role models we can. Everything else they can learn over time, but no one else will provide this understanding as a living embodiment. I understood this even more deeply from launching my Sacred Feminine course years ago. One of the assignments I gave my students was to write out their earliest feminine and masculine role models and what they learned from them. It was such an eye-opening experience for me to read the answers. It made me realize how important these roles are and how not having healthy models sets you up for failure in relationships later. My students are high achieving, "successful" women who never learned how the healthy masculine and feminine behaves in relationships. This is the most important gift we have given our children. Making our own embodiment and our marriage a priority is our best parenting hack.

CHAPTER *Seven*
BE A BITCH ONCE

As I started creating and living a life of alignment of my deepest desires, I suddenly became a "safe place" for people who are lost in life. There would be no problem with this if they were healthy people looking for inspiration and motivation. Often, I was attracting jealousy and envy and people who wanted to disrupt my newfound family and peace. Forgetting that my own family and peace should be my number one priority, I started helping some of these people. Their urgency suddenly became my priority, sending me into the very familiar guilt, shame, over-giving, and people-pleasing patterns that I had learned from my parents. It seemed I still had a lot more inner work to do.

One of the terrible womb wounds and conditioning I received from my childhood was that of people-pleasing and toxic giving. Toxic giving is when you give at your expense out of obligation, guilt, shame, or some other nonsense story you or society has created. It's not the feel good, expansive type of giving that generates from a person's sheer joy and overflow. It became really clear to me that if I was going to prioritize my own peace and my family's health, I was going to have to learn a new way of being.

I had no concept of the word "boundaries" at this time in my life, but knew I had to figure out a way to be able to say no and stick to it no matter how much guilt or shame I was subjected to. In short, I was going to learn how to be savage fast! One of the savage techniques I decided to try is actually something I learned from my culture. It doesn't translate quite exactly in this way but there's a concept of "being bad once". An aunt used this once and I was so intrigued! Needless to say, it has changed my life and my clients love it! I have renamed it the "Be a Bitch Once" technique.

This technique has been used over and over again in my life to keep myself and my family at the center of my priority. In the world that we live today with its many distractions and imaginary emergencies, Being a Bitch Once has been life saving. So, let's say that your friend or relative needs a place to stay and despite that deep feeling of doom in your gut, you let them come stay with you for a couple of days while they figure things out.

They come over to your house and now they are complaining about the food, being mean to your husband and kids, and making a lot of noise at night when it's your family's bedtime. Your family expects you to go and have a talk with them every time they do something outside the norm of your family's house culture. Obviously, your relative does not appreciate your talks or your house rules. Now that you said "yes" to them, you have to be a bitch so many times.

You become a bitch every time you have to explain to them that they have to clean up after themselves. You have to explain to them that no they cannot have guests come over. You have to explain to them that they can't play loud music after it's your kid's bedtime. Do you see where this is going? I can't tell you how many times I have had to be a bitch one million times because of getting myself into these situations. So, when I remembered this concept from my culture, I created a whole new set of personal values and I decided that I was only going to Be the Bitch, Once. Say no the first time!

Now this sounds easier said than done for someone raised with so many people-pleasing tendencies. However, having to Be a Bitch Once is definitely easier than having to fix things when you have already allowed certain behaviors. Despite the title of this technique, you don't have to be mean or rude when saying no. Think of it as collapsing the complaints. Being a Bitch Once means the only complaint anyone can have about you is that you said no. That's it. It never goes any further than that.

So, in this scenario, you wouldn't have to be a bitch one million times in correcting your family member and in all the things that you had to do if you just simply said, "*hey actually I'm sorry I can't let you stay with me.*" Now I'm not saying don't do charity or help people out. I am a very generous person and I love being charitable but I also try to do it from my overflow. There is a big difference between helping someone and enabling them. Help them in ways that feel good, not make you resentful and then jeopardize the long term relationship.

Years ago, my therapist pointed out that I had the tendency to keep saying yes when I really needed to say no, until I felt like I had no choice but to completely destroy the relationship to get myself out of that situation! She nailed it! I had a unique gift of turning even the kindest people into what seemed like predators by over-giving and saying yes to things I didn't really want to do! And then of course blame them for taking advantage of me even though I had allowed it all along.

You get to choose how you design your life. In this case, Being a Bitch Once is saying no the first time. Oddly enough, I have preserved way more relationships by Being a Bitch Once than by trying to be nice. Try it, it's a game changer and a savage requirement for the top 1% woman you are destined to become.

People-Pleasing Over-Correction #1

Overcorrect for your people-pleasing tendencies by saying "no" to most requests. The truth is that you can always go back and say "yes" later if you change your mind. The other way around doesn't go over too well. If your current habit is to say "yes" to everything without giving yourself space and time to think it over and then regret it later, this is a much bigger problem.

There was a study done with chimps (our closest relatives in the animal kingdom) where they were perfectly happy and content and then the researchers gave them each two apples. Now the chimps were over the moon with happiness and excitement! A few moments later, the researchers took away one apple from the chimps. As you can imagine they were now livid, even though they still had one apple when moments ago they had none. Their standards and expectations had now changed and they wanted both apples. So, when we say "yes" and then take that away, people tend to get upset. However, if you say "no" and later change your mind, that will be a welcome surprise for them.

In my early 20s, I became more independent and started earning good money, but I didn't have the proper boundaries in place yet. I ended up co-signing a car for a family member and of course ended up making most of the payments. So, when my parents suggested I put their mortgage in my name to get them a better rate, I had to learn to be a bitch quickly! I loved my parents but was not ready to put their house in my name. They had a history of making crazy money decisions and I knew this was going to not only destroy my credit but also our relationship. So, I said, "no." They were upset for a few weeks and then got over it. You train people how to treat you.

People-Pleasing Over-Correction #2

We discussed this in a previous chapter, but honestly, it's worth repeating here. Yes, it's that important! Be consistent in your decisions with everyone. Don't have a different set of rules for your mom and a different set for your mother-in-law. We set ourselves up for manipulation when we try to make up an answer on the fly depending on who is asking and what their situation is. I saw this play out with Sheena and myself hundreds of times! People will figure out exactly what to say and how to say it to get their hands in your pocket. They might even send over the person who you tend to say yes to more often to ask on their behalf. Children are especially very good at this! Once people figured out the answer is no regardless of who is asking and when, it became a part of my identity and they stopped messing around.

People respect you more when you are honest and upfront of what works and what doesn't work for you. Sure, some people may be mad at you but honestly the only ones upset at your boundaries are often the ones breaking them. One thing I have learned is that boundaries start energetically first. I call this "Boundaries In." "Boundaries in" are structures that contain the flow of love. Boundaries out is when we think other people are at fault for not honoring boundaries and therefore we must keep them out. I used to think this way when I had no boundaries and liked to pretend it was everyone else's fault. Then I realized I wasn't trying to keep anyone out. I was trying to keep me in.

I started seeing boundaries as a silent, internal decision and knowing. Once I started setting boundaries with myself first, it actually eliminated the need to discuss my boundaries with other people. Human boundaries are often "boundaries out" and translate into pushing people away and out. Spiritual boundaries are "boundaries in" and translate into "I am being honest about what works and doesn't work so that we can have a better relationship." We all get to have options and stay in our zones of pleasure.

Being a Bitch Once is about radical honesty of what works and doesn't work for you. Do it the first time and it will save you so much time, energy, and money! The most difficult part of this has been overcoming cultural and familial expectations and norms. In my culture, people will guilt and shame you into things and then once they are "in", it's hard to get yourself out of it. They may even make the entire situation that they got into suddenly your fault. The nicer you are, the more uncomfortable situations you will be put in. Learning to say "NO" has been one of my highest income and life skill sets I have learned to embody!

Here are the three types of people to look out for and use the Be a Bitch Once technique immediately on. Type one is someone who constantly compliments you on everything you do for them and how generous you are. This is to manipulate you into doing more. Men are even more susceptible to this because they love being seen as a hero. However, as someone whose primary love language is words of admiration, I have fallen for this more times than I care to admit.

The solution for me is to drop in and be brutally honest if I really want to give or do what is being requested. Don't let the praise and need to be seen in a positive light get you into tricky situations. Understand that your need for validation is the reason you get into these situations. Take care of the core wound and give yourself the validation you desperately want from others.

The second type of person to beware of is the complainer. This person will always complain about how anything you or someone else does is not enough. I have encountered many people who complained about support, gifts, donations, etc. My immediate response would be to think they probably complain to others about the gifts I have given them as well! Complaining is the easiest way to get me to stop giving you anything. My go-to response for this is to agree with everything they are saying and then stop giving anything more. People who have trouble receiving a little will not be able to suddenly receive a lot. It's an illusion for them to think if you only gave them more than they would have enough. **They do not have the ability to receive**. Don't waste your resources! Invest that money in your future and children's legacy.

The third type of person to look out for is anyone who inserts themselves into your life and starts doing you favors you don't want them to do. You might be tempted to be nice and let them give to you, but this is a trap! They will do things for you that you don't want or need, tell the whole world about their generosity, and guilt you into doing things for them that you also don't want to do! Can you see how manipulative this is? Here is the kicker: A lot of these people don't realize they are doing this. At least that's what I have convinced myself over the years.

I had an aunt that would go out of her way to do things for you, give you expensive gifts, cook for you, and invite you over all the time. She would also learn all your secrets, spread rumors about you, and insert herself into your family business, often causing massive rifts between people. She would get you so indebted in favors, that you didn't need or ask for, and then have her way with you! I learned to decline her "generosity" the first time around.

Lesson: Be a Bitch Once so you don't have to be a bitch many times. Be consistent in your "NOs" and soon enough it will become a part of your identity and you will no longer be seen as a validation seeking junkie and people pleaser!

Journal Prompts:

Where in my life did I try playing the nice girl and then end up being a bitch many times?

Where in my life can I Be a Bitch Once so I don't have to be a bitch many times?

How will Being a Bitch Once actually heal and support my relationships?

Inner Work: Write out the following statements in your journal and see what comes up. These statements have helped me gain clarity on my new boundaries in life.

"I am no longer available for…"

"I am now open to receive…"

Drowning People Drown People

I used to be deathly afraid of bodies of water and therefore never learned how to swim in childhood. As an adult, I would lay by the pool or just put my feet in when out with the family. And then I heard something that changed my entire perspective about my fear. When someone is drowning, their human "survival at all costs" instincts kick in. They will then attempt to use anything and everything they can to save themselves. Drowning people or even someone who thinks they are drowning may grab on to other people, even children around them to keep themselves from drowning. As the mother of three young kids at the time I heard this, this scared me more than my fear of water. I learned to swim in under a week after hearing this truth.

When I shared this on my YouTube channel, I was flooded with stories from women who had experienced this. Someone literally tried to save themselves while holding them under water for support! I have found this to be a great metaphor for how others can also energetically drown you. Stay away from drowning people, or at the very least, keep a healthy distance.

They will drown you if you try to save them without getting yourself to safety first.

I have experienced this first hand many times in my life and path to success. My parents used to believe that some people are unlucky for you. Something about their stars and your stars not aligning. This doesn't mean they are bad people. Just that they don't belong in your inner circle. Since they can't come with you, they will try to drown you to keep you down at their level.

I didn't take this too seriously until it started playing out in my life. Once I was safely at shore, i.e. married and finally starting to feel safe in my body, an old friend reached out for help. She had a habit of getting herself in crazy situations and everything inside of me said not to let her back into my life. Unfortunately, I didn't listen to my intuition. I can't even begin to tell you how much trouble she ended up causing in my life. As soon as she came back, it was like the old Mina with the lower consciousness also came back. I had to do another level of inner work around boundaries and giving others so much access to me and my family. I had to have some very uncomfortable conversations. The minute she was out of my life, my life quantum leaped again, actually to even bigger and better levels! Probably as a result of my newfound personal power and new inner work.

I have had to do this layer of inner work enough times in my life to know this: You can't help everyone. As painful as it might be, see them as capable and wish them well. Pray for their success even, but you don't need to step into the savior role just because they showed up. People-pleasing, needing validation of your self-worth, and mining for constant appreciation from others are some of the reasons we fall into these traps. I'm all for helping our friends or family members during a hard time. But not if it's a constant pattern in their life. That can be a huge red flag of their lack of ability to take personal responsibility for their life and success.

Remember: People will keep creating problems if you keep bailing them out. Let them surprise you and themselves by figuring it out. I have come to realize these hardships in life activate codes and consciousness that contribute to our growth and expansion. When we step in and temper with someone's experience of life, we actually stunt their growth. Provide them with emotional support and encouragement. Be there for them in emotional support from a distance. Cheer them on. But don't take over for them living their life. And if needed, give them the energetic finger.

Sheena's Infamous Energetic Finger

I once heard someone say that there are as many versions of you as there are people who have laid eyes on you. So, if you have encountered 10,000 people in your life, there are 10,000 versions of you. Each person has created a version of you in their mind's eye that may have absolutely nothing to do with the actual, real you. This means there are millions of opinions or versions of you out there that have nothing to do with you. Most of these opinions we will never encounter or hear about. They are literally none of our business. The only time we make it our business is when we have the need to defend or justify someone else's opinion about us. Don't do it, there is no point. Their concept of you has nothing to actually do with you.

My mother had this hilarious way of giving people the finger when they turned around to walk away after sharing their unsolicited opinions or advice on how she should or shouldn't live her life. I will admit that I used to be really embarrassed about her doing this. If you know anything about immigrant moms, they can't be controlled and Sheena always did Sheena! Years later, I actually started using her obnoxious technique, albeit only "energetically" and it was so deeply healing! That's where the concept of "give them the energetic finger" came from. What the energetic finger does is remove your emotional involvement or entanglement with other people's opinions. It's such a transformative, and releasing concept in my life.

Sheena used to say that if you want to get someone to stop giving you unsolicited advice, ask them for money. Most will run away, and if they gave you money then they just paid you to pretend to listen to their nonsense advice. All I know is that none of these people showed up giving me any money or any sort of concern about how I was going to survive in life. Not even fake concern, but, yes, they had a lot of opinions about my life decisions and my life choices. So, I simply stopped caring and gave them the energetic finger. My new motto was: If you are not paying my bills, your opinion doesn't matter.

We are biologically designed to care about what other people think of us. However, that doesn't mean we care what everyone thinks of us. Clearly define who the most important people are and weigh in their opinions against your own. Typically, we care most about potential mates, family, friends, and trade partners (people we do business with in some way). Asking everyone for validation is level 10 cray. You are not a parking ticket. Stop trying to get validated. Define your tribe and don't worry about other random opinions.

Always remember: The most important opinion in your life is your own opinion of yourself. Are you happy with your decisions and actions in life? If not, correct them. Make a great impression of yourself in your own mind and your self-esteem will rise as a reflection of that. One way to know if you are happy with your life decisions is to gauge if you get triggered when someone questions them. When we are 100% sure and confident about our own decisions, we don't care much about others' opinions about them.

You know that I have spent a lot of time being a Self-Aware Barbie, and because of that, I am not one to lie to myself or pretend like I actually value myself when I don't. So, I have gone to evolution to understand why we behave the way we do. Why do we bash and second guess ourselves so much? Why don't we have natural confidence and self-esteem?

The answer was not only understandable but also so simple to implement. Honestly one of the best concepts I've learned about self-esteem is about our internal audience. I talked about this in my first book,

Contained in Love, but will go over it briefly here. It's that important. We have evolved to have this internal audience that judges how we will be perceived by an imaginary tribe. Tribes have been very important to our survival and upsetting members of the tribe could mean life and death for our ancestors. The internal audience is a self-rehearsal mechanism. This mechanism developed because we couldn't rehearse in public without our tribe members seeing and hearing us. Our internal audience judges our behavior based on how it perceives other people will judge us. Our self-esteem is created from this analysis from our internal audience.

For example, if I feel like I am overweight, and my internal audience deems this to lower my social status or mate value, it will judge me super harshly in hopes that I do something about it. If every Monday I go on a diet and every Wednesday I forget about the diet, my internal audience will be judging me very harshly. It honestly thinks it's saving me from being kicked out of the tribe by warning me first. Isn't evolution wonderful in its own crazy way?

Every time I look in the mirror, it's going to remind me how fat I am and how I can't keep any diet and I shouldn't eat that and how I'm out of control. So, the solution to this is actually convincing your internal audience that you are a person of integrity and will not be kicked out of the tribe. This is the formula that determines our self-esteem. How we show up and what kind of effect we put into pleasing the internal audience determines our self-esteem.

Here is my formula for pleasing the internal audience (IA) which is the secret evolutionary hack for having self-esteem.

Listen to your IA and make a note of the things they are unhappy about. Choose the biggest area. Break down the thing into the smallest doable chunks. So, for example, let's say I choose fitness. Which I actually did by the way when my daughter was born. I knew I couldn't work out an hour a day with three kids and bad knees from my previous rheumatoid arthritis damage. I had tried that before and failed. So, I decided to only work out five minutes a day in the beginning. At first my internal audience was very skeptical. "*You will quit in a day or two,*" it mirrored back to me.

"*There is no way you will keep doing this.*" But by the fourth or fifth day, it stopped being skeptical. In fact, by the following week, it was cheering me on because it started gaining confidence in my abilities to see this through. So after about a week or two of this I raised the bar to 10 minutes a day. Now my internal audience was a little skeptical again, but after I did that for a few more days it realized, "*oh she's actually going to do this.*"

It's been about 10 years now and I've been consistently working out for 20 minutes a day at least four to five times a week. Now all of the things that I have promised my internal audience I have done and because of that I have a bunch of cheerleaders in my head.

Every time I look in the mirror, all I hear is "*Wow, you're so beautiful. You look so great.*" Your internal audience is basically just responding to your own internal integrity and this is one of the biggest hacks that you can use to actually turn your negative thoughts into positive affirmations. Instead of having trolls in your mind, you now have a whole bunch of cheerleaders.

And this is how to have confidence and self-esteem in any area of your life.

Lesson: They are not you and you are not them. Give them and their opinions the energetic finger and keep it moving. Decide to actually do something about the negative voices in your head and take action to improve your life.

Journal Prompts:

Who is currently taking up rent free residence in my mind and needs the energetic finger?

____

____

____

What is my internal audience currently saying? How can I listen to it using the self-esteem hack and turn it into my personal cheerleading squad?

____

____

____

Turn one intention into small daily actions and then follow it! Literally, it's that easy to create confidence!

I Want You to Shut Up

Talking is the cheapest, largely inefficient way of releasing pressure built up from trapped energy. It's inefficient because the core energy is still left trapped inside our body. This is why so many people run their mouths but actually say very little of value. This is also why Self-Aware Barbies give so much unsolicited advice. The pressure created from all the new information, sometimes left unembodied, needs to be spit out unto others.

Every time you open your mouth, you reveal important information about yourself, your thoughts, your feelings, your intentions and so much more. Some women talk as an excuse to "speak their truth" and "stand up for themselves." No one cares and they are now gathering data about you that you are volunteering. If you actually had some boundaries, your silence would speak like thunder. You can say way more with less words with the right energy than lots of words with the wrong energy.

Ration the words and amplify the energy. This is hard to do because it requires a great deal of self-awareness and emotional control. Both of which are high income skill sets, by the way. Few people truly process them and therefore they speak to the true power of the ones that embody this.

Emotional control comes from emotional intelligence. We used to believe there was only one type of intelligence. You either had it or you didn't. We now know there are many types of intelligence, emotional being one of the rarest, in my opinion. In order to have more emotional control, you must first release the emotions causing you to speak without self-awareness. This is fairly easy to do and you will find my simple process below. Having more space within our emotional body helps us stop and discern what we are about to say before we react. This is just an important aspect of being an evolved, conscious being.

Our triggers are emotional wounds very similar to physical wounds. When someone brushes past a physical wound, we might scream in pain. Triggers are the emotional equivalent to physical wounds. If something triggers you, it means it pushed up against the emotional wound and caused you pain. Heal the wound and you won't be triggered.

Here is a simple process.

Every time you are triggered, instead of speaking, go towards the sensations happening inside your body. All emotions cause sensational responses inside our body. Some are very faint, while others cause bigger ripples or even roller coasters. Sensations can show up as tightness, burning, swirling, butterflies, heaviness, or a feeling of constriction.

Where you feel these sensations varies from body to body and even trigger to trigger within the same body. Once located, sit with the sensation with no agenda. Let the communication signal of the trigger realize you have received the message. Let it be received with love. Talking, screaming, lashing out are all distractions from the actual purpose of the trigger.

Let it be seen, heard, and loved in silence. Let the purpose of speaking be to connect, inspire, love, and admire.

The Eyes are not a Camera, They are a Projector

People see what they want to see. This means there are billions of realities out there. Each one being seen from the eyes of the beholder. Think of everyone's perception as their own mental movie. They are the main character in their world and everyone else either plays a supporting role or is an extra. When two people interact, they are experiencing and telling the story from their movie.

Perceptions are actually fun house mirrors and distort reality based on each person's bias, values, filters, and stories. This is why there is absolutely no need to get worked up about someone else's perceptions about reality. Next time you find yourself getting all worked up about someone else's perception, remind yourself that it's their story and they have a right to it.

Successful relationships actually depend on two people being able to maintain their own mental movie as a lead star and being a co-star in their partner's movie. This is true in all relationships, not just romantic ones. People who have trouble starring in someone else's movie while maintaining their own will have issues in relationships.

For example, I am the main character in my own movie, while being a co-star in my husband and children's individual movies. This is a wonderful dance we all play and understanding this has been so useful. It helps us honor each other's movies while also honoring our own.

The Various Dimensions of Boundaries

Creating Boundaries in various dimensions has been a game changer for my emotional and physical well-being. Here is a quick guide to how I define layers of boundaries. Understanding boundaries on the various dimensions has really helped me understand them. I used to be someone that really struggled in this area, mainly because I didn't have any and expected others to uphold my imaginary, non-existent boundaries!

One interesting thing about my boundary journey is that I rarely need to communicate my boundaries with others. This one was shocking since so many people recommend sitting others down and having a talk with them about what is and is not acceptable. This never seemed to work for me. However, my dimensional process of setting boundaries rarely needs boundaries to be verbally communicated. Although I may at times communicate my desire.

Emotional Boundaries: How I FEEL about something. What I will let get to me. The price of my peace. Over the years of doing my inner work, what will get me "hot and bothered" has changed from - "pretty much anything" to "pretty much NOTHING!" And boy what a relief this has been! When I think of emotional boundaries - I think of the insides of my body. This is kind of similar to upgrading your problems which we discussed in chapter three. Upgrade what gets your emotional energy by setting emotional boundaries. These are boundaries we set with ourselves and don't really need to discuss with anyone else which is one of my most favorite things!

Another way I use emotional boundaries in my life is my "remove emotions out of it" technique. There are things in life that get complicated when we add emotions to them that are otherwise really easy. Dating is one of those areas of life. Business also requires us to get out of our emotions to work efficiently. Notice where in your life you are making it way more complicated by adding emotions. Try doing the same tasks by removing emotions out of it and see if it's any easier.

Physical Boundaries: What I will and will not allow in my space and life experience. I like my space clean and clutter free. I like to hang out with up-lifting or at the very least, neutral people. I will not waste precious time with negative people, jealous people, or people who bring others down. I also like to create time and space for solitude - which I call my «being with the Divine time.» Spending time in solitude can help us determine and reset ourselves from what is "ours" and what needs to be returned to sender. Physical boundaries also include how much time I spend with whom. This can also define work time versus family time for some people.

Energetic Boundaries: This work began with first becoming aware of how much masculine vs feminine energy I was running through my body at any given time. This awareness CHANGED THE GAME! Having the freedom and awareness to change my energy at will was everything! The next layer for me as an empath (highly sensitive person) was to build my resilience. The ability to bounce back after energetic setbacks. Faster and faster each time. The final layer was DECIDING what I was and wasn›t available for energetically. The day you decide on a new energetic boundary - the world realigns to meet you there.

Energetic Boundaries

Energetic boundaries have impacted my life the most and I would like to spend a little more time explaining these. Energetic boundaries are internal decisions and commitments we make and keep with ourselves. My favorite part about these types of boundaries is the fact that I don't have to communicate them with other people and they give me all the control. Personally, every energetic boundary has started with the following statement (ahem, sometimes said in a very passionate way).

"*I am no longer available for...*" Being energetically available for something keeps us engaging and entangling with it whilst taking little to no personal responsibility for our part in the dynamic. Once I set the energetic boundary of no longer being available for something, it's amazing to me how fast that thing disappears from my reality. Our attention, awareness, and energetic investment often keeps things or situations we have outgrown lingering in our world.

Some examples from my personal life:

"*I am no longer available for giving unsolicited advice to people and then feeling unappreciated.*" This led to me no longer giving unsolicited advice and honoring my work by engaging compensation from those who truly wanted to learn from me.

"*I am no longer available for being disrespected in my own home.*" This one led to me not inviting disrespectful family and friends over to my home instead of trying to get them to behave in ways they weren't willing to do.

"*I am no longer available for earning peanuts for my sacred work.*" This led me to raise my prices to what is most aligned at my current stage of expertise and consciousness.

As you can see, each of these energetic boundary decisions and statements were followed up with taking the appropriate aligned actions of course, but without the energetic boundary in place first, all actions would have been fruitless.

In the first example, I stopped giving people unsolicited advice and therefore was no longer feeling unappreciated. You see how easy it was. Previously, I had tried to get people who didn't want my advice to appreciate me and trust me. That was much harder.

In the second example, I stopped letting disrespectful friends and family members in my home. In fact, most of those people aren't even in my life anymore. The daily drama and emotional rollercoasters were literally keeping me away from my eight-figure life! We don't have unlimited emotional energy. It's really best to channel ours in ways that will serve our life experience the most. Have you ever imagined what that emotional energy could be used to create instead?

In the third example, I raised my prices and let the clients who didn't want to pay the new prices fall away. You would be surprised how much more people value your work and services when you value your work and services.

Journal Prompts:

What are my current emotional boundaries? Do they serve where I am going or do they need to be updated?

What are my current physical boundaries? Do they serve where I am going or do they need to be updated?

What are my current energetic boundaries? Do they serve where I am going or do they need to be updated?

Queens don't D.I.Y

The inner work processes I have shared so far have changed my life personally on levels beyond words. Having said that, there came a time in my journey when I needed more support. I am a woman who has gone through some serious real life stuff. Some of which I have shared in the previous chapters, and some too traumatizing to revisit for any of us. As I was evolving from the Self-Aware Barbie stage into the Million Dollar Stage, life threw me a curveball. There had been an incident with a family member that had triggered an intense fear response in my nervous system. Her behavior was so out of the ordinary and sudden that it left me really confused. I started having nightmares and anxiety and wanted to quit my business.

It was a little confusing to me why I suddenly wanted to withdraw from my business as a result of this event. I could feel that this issue wasn't something I could work with on my own. I leaned on my husband, children, and close friends for support while taking a break from YouTube. Something told me there was a huge awakening coming at the end of this. As always, I asked God for support. I needed some tools that I didn't have in my toolbox.

"*Dear God, I am handing over this problem to you, please show me the way.*"

I was soon led into therapy. A part of me was resisting the process because I had already done so much inner work on myself at this point. However, I never deny God's requests. I worked with my first therapist for two months. She said I was exhibiting symptoms of PTSD and that's why I wanted to withdraw from anything that could trigger me further like YouTube. She suggested EMDR (Eye Movement Desensitization and Reprocessing) therapy. I soon connected with another therapist who understood energy and many of the principals I talked about on my channel. I knew this was the right person for me!

I worked with her for several months. The EMDR was a simple but sometimes scary process but I believe it truly healed me from my deeper childhood trauma. It was like my personal inner work loosened the jar, and the EMDR completely released it! I am really blessed to not only be surrounded by my loving family, but also have manifested such amazing therapists who supported me through this difficult point in my journey. They both reminded me of the big things I am here to do, be, create and celebrate everything I had already created as well.

Could you imagine how long it would have taken me, if ever, to heal from my PTSD if I hadn't asked for support? A lifelong of playing small was avoided through a few months of commitment into a supportive container.

Lesson: Be willing to ask for support. We don't have to do it all by ourselves.

Journal Prompts:

Where in my life do I truly need support but am trying to DIY it?

How will having support help me collapse time and quantum leap my progress?

Where in my life am I not allowing or receiving the support I desire?

What would happen if I surrendered to being supported?

Are my current beliefs around support, expanding me or contracting my growth?

Toxic People

The truth is that toxic people have existed from the dawn of time. We could simply choose to avoid them, which is something I have certainly done in the past. Every time I would end relationships with toxic friends, another person would manifest in my reality exhibiting the same exact dynamics. I wondered if I had a kick me sign on my back that I couldn't see. The unfortunate answer is "yes, I did!" It was an energetic invitation, not a physical sign. Until I actually sat down to decipher (mostly in my journal) my own personal contribution to the dynamic and take 100% responsibility for what I was co-creating, nothing changed.

Once I saw why and how I was deliberately, yet unknowingly attracting and then choosing such dynamics, I was able to manifest myself out of them! This is why I don't waste time blaming other people for anything. Yes, I take the actions I need to take to report crimes, create boundaries, distance, and protect myself in any and every way I need to. But I don't waste time blaming. That time and energy can be used to learn the lessons, change my inputs, which then changes the outputs of my reality. I am a woman who takes 100% responsibility for my life. Yes, not everything is in our control, but how we react and choose to move forward is something we control.

I may not have contributed to the wounds I have incurred in my life, especially not the ones that happened in childhood, but I am the one that decides whether I heal or not. That is something that is my responsibility, duty, and birthright.

CHAPTER *Eight*
WEALTHY WOMAN ERA BEGINS

Google: "*Why is everyone being so nice to me suddenly.*" I entered these exact words into my Google search bar right as I was entering the Million Dollar Babe phase. I was legitimately confused. I had given person after person the energetic finger, stopped giving people advice, let toxic people go from my life, and set boundary after boundary. Shouldn't everyone be mad at me? Why was everyone suddenly treating me better? Men were noticing me more than ever, even with my three kids in tow! People were being respectful of my time. Children were smiling at me, and even the bird songs seemed more melodious. I seemed lighter and softer, even to myself. And the most noticeable difference, I had much less anxiety, no more panic attacks, and I was talking a lot less. Life felt really really good. Even ecstatic at moments. What was happening to me?

Between each season of life, there is an intersection of identity. If you see each stage as a separate and distinct identity inside of you, you will see the emergence of five or even more different versions of you. Sometimes women can really struggle at that intersection of identities, for example when they leave the education stage into dating for marriage. Or the marriage stage into motherhood. Each transition brings its own life lessons, challenges, doubts, awakenings, and ascension process. At each phase you may need to revisit your core beliefs and see how they match the new identity you are stepping into. For those of us doing inner work in addition to following our seasons of life, there are additional intersections, the ones between the four stages I outlined in chapter three.

Being in our Basic Babe and Self-Aware Barbie stages is really hard on us physically, emotionally, and energetically. It uses up a lot of resources to stay at this level of density. I didn't know this at the time, but I was entering my Million Dollar Babe era that day when I entered those words in the Google search bar. Without the constant to-do lists, drama with friends and family members, and low grade anxiety running behind the scenes, the whispers of the soul become loud and crystalline clear. My intuition was getting stronger, and I could feel my body in ways like never before. I was at the intersection of identities. At that moment, the Million Dollar Babe was awakening inside of me but I still had the muscle memory of the Self-Aware Barbie. It would be years until these four stages would even appear in my meditation and become the foundation of my sacred work. So, I had no idea what was happening but it felt absolutely fantastic!

Everything I have shared with you so far has played a huge role in clearing emotional, energetic, and physical space in my psyche and life. All of these processes, techniques, and downloads have helped me get the "human" out of the way to connect with my divinity. The strangest thing that happened during this time was when my past memories started unlocking. I was always noted with saying that I had a bad memory. I had blocked off huge chunks of my childhood due to childhood trauma. As I was stepping into the Million Dollar Babe stage, all of a sudden, I started unlocking wonderful memories of my parents instead of only remembering my resentments towards my childhood.

Past memories of my father being there for me. Of all the sacrifices Sheena has made for our family and others. I started to do deep forgiveness work so I could fully erase any lingering resentments I had towards my parents. I used my forgiveness meditation in my Love Light Mediations program. Memories reside in the creative part of our brain. This means we make up at least 50% of our memories and take a lot of creative liberties for the other 50%. I had blocked off the good times I had with my family because they didn't match the story of my childhood trauma. Doing my inner work changed my past as I started unlocking a more holistic view of my childhood instead of only remembering the bad times.

This is why inner work is so important, it changes not only our present and our future, it rewrites our past as well. Being at the intersection of identities was no easy task. This is the junction at which we tend to self-sabotage the most. The muscle memory of the old self often pulls at the consciousness of the self we are becoming. Even though I had cleared massive space in my life through my new energetic boundaries and awakening consciousness, I found myself being pulled back into the old self many times.

I prayed about it and asked for guidance and soon a clear next path was shown to me. Instead of creating drama, I was asked to immerse myself into what was revealed to me as Sacred Service. God was asking me to use what I had learned to help others. Although that excited me, I also felt a lot of imposter syndrome. Imposter syndrome is the inability to see yourself as qualified or worthy of what you have achieved. I asked for another sign and several people on my existing YouTube channel started mentioning Life Coaching.

I started my YouTube channel in January of 2011, about eight months after Sheena passed away. It was my strange way of grieving. I wanted to connect with other women and also keep myself busy. I wasn't sure if I was dealing with postpartum depression, simply grieving or both, but I knew I needed to snap myself out of it. I had started sharing hauls, which quickly led me to share helpful advice on things I was learning or working on in my personal life. In that short week after I asked the Universe for a sign, three people mentioned in the comments that I should be a life coach. I had no idea what this meant.

"*What is a life coach?*" I asked my husband.

He pulled out his phone, typed something and replied, "*Wow, this sounds exactly like you.*"

That evening I had enrolled in a Life Coaching Certification course. I was already overqualified with my university degree, but felt like I should at least learn what life coaching was. I was certified within the week. I went on YouTube to announce that I had become a Life Coach, as they requested, and that day I had my first 10 clients.

It felt so good to be helping people and making my own money again! I had forgotten how good it feels to create something of your own. And the best part was I didn't have to leave my home. Keeping busy doing something that came so naturally to me helped me leave the muscle memory of the Self-Aware Barbie and step deeper into the Million Dollar Babe.

Resting Deeper than Habit

Embodiment is the energetic, emotional, and physical memorization of new datasets and then using epigenetics to encode them into your DNA structures. It's when the information turns into a code that dictates your way of being. It's when something stops being "hard" and becomes natural. The biggest difference between the Self-Aware Barbie and Million Dollar Babe is embodiment. Our Self-Aware Barbie relies on conscious and unconscious habits. The MDB rests deeper than habit, in embodiment.

Embodiment is when the information you have gathered has been memorized by your body. It has become a part of your daily habits, and most importantly, your identity. Instead of knowing the thing, you have become the thing. I would like to share my embodiment process with you. Keep in mind that when we list out any process, it can seem kind of daunting or like "a lot of work." In the beginning it may be a lot of steps to work through, but eventually your subconscious automates the process and you do it with little effort or thought. Just like when you first started riding your bike, swimming, or driving. It all took effort until it suddenly didn't. All of my processes now run behind the scenes of my awareness. And the same will happen for you.

My Embodiment Process:

Step #1. State your desire: What do I truly desire to embody?

Step #2. Core beliefs: Does anything need updating for me to be able to embody this?

How does this fit into my personal values? What parts of my identity need to be updated?

What energy do I need to have for this to be my new reality?

What do I need to get rid of from my life for this to have the space that it needs?

What daily actions do I need to take? How can I break this down into small, digestible steps that compound over time?

What is the high hanging fruit here that gives me elite level, top 1% advantage?

Step #3. Repeat consistently for long periods of time.

In my SAB days, it took me 6-18 months to embody something and also trust myself to have embodied it. Over the years, as my own inner work and ability to trust myself with full faith has compounded, I am able to embody things in weeks or even days. Everything you invest in yourself compounds over time, creating exponential results.

Here is an embodiment exercise:

Elevator Embodiment Exercise:

Close your eyes. Imagine there is an elevator in your head. Notice that it says you are on the 10th floor. Get into the elevator and hit the basement button. Slowly go vertically down your body until the elevator stops and opens in your womb space.

Get out and look around. What do you notice? How do you feel? Are the sensations here different from the 10th floor? Refrain from accessing your brain to answer any of these questions.

You left your brain on the 10th floor. You are now in the basement.

During the day - anytime you find yourself getting too "heady" - take the elevator down and access the womb's wisdom to make your decisions. Journal on the sensations and inner workings. Your assignment in the MDB stage is faith, surrender, and pleasure. These are often misunderstood concepts so let's explain them a bit further.

The Million Dollar Babe

Why does our wealthy woman era begin after unlocking the Million Dollar Babe stage? In order to understand this, we must first understand how creation works. In order to create anything, we need both the masculine and feminine energies. Both the metaphorical egg and sperm. In the SAB stage, we are mostly in our masculine energy. Creating matter from matter. We are leaving God's divine plan and our metaphysical self out of the equation. How far can you really get with half of you cut off?

Well, it turns out modern day women can get pretty far even with a whole half of them missing! However, as we have discussed before, there is an emotional, energetic, and physical cost to doing it the hard way. Imagine how much further you can go with all of you in attendance. The SAB is trapped in the world of logic and reason. Which can only take you so far because you are not accessing the heart's wisdom and soul's knowing of your divine purpose.

In the MDB stage, we start using both our left and right brain at the same time. We start using our hands and feet in collaboration with our heart, soul, and most of all, God! Your desires, spirituality, and metaphysical guidance is the feminine realm of creation. You taking aligned action and moving your hands and feet are the masculine part of creation.

Every single exercise, journal prompt, and embodiment practice I have given you in this book has been helping you leave the mental plane and access more and more of your metaphysical self. No one practice may seem ground-breaking on its own, but collectively they start breaking our addictions to suffering, and expanding our nervous system to access the quantum field of metaphysical wisdom. All of this inner work compounds over time. It becomes your new way of being. Your new normal.

JOURNAL PROMPTS:

In what ways is my masculine side currently supporting me?

In what ways is my feminine side currently supporting me?

What areas of my life need more feminine energy?

What areas of my life need more masculine energy?

How can these two energies work better together to create a beautiful life experience for me?

Faith

Faith is a decision I made decades ago and automated. It's one of my personal values. Faith just is. It's never a question whether I will have faith or not. It's already been decided. I have faith in the Divine. I have faith in God's order. I also have faith in myself to figure it out. To learn, grow, evolve, and find the blessings in everything life presents at me. When students ask me how to have faith, my response is always, decide to have faith. Choose into it daily and you will embody it in no time.

Faith is one of those equalizer energies. Whether you are rich or poor, tall or short, you have equal access to deciding to have faith. I have seen people have faith in the worst of situations and decide not to when everything is relatively good. Your circumstances or situations don't determine your faith, you determine your faith. Our brains have automated fear as a result of our evolutionary history, it's only fair we give faith equal footing by automating it as well.

I wonder how different your life would be if you automated faith like our brains have automated fear. Could you imagine the possibilities? How much emotional energy would you save from having your emotional set point set to faith instead of fear!

Surrender

"Mina, isn't it easier for you to surrender because you are married to a good, kind man?"

I was a bit confused when a student posted this question. What did my husband have to do with my ability to surrender? After thinking about it for a moment, I realized she didn't understand what surrender really meant.

"*Surrender is not a response,*" I wrote back. "*It's an embodiment.*"

Let me explain. I do not surrender to people. Yes, not even my husband, as wonderful as he is. I simply surrender. On a physical level, this means I drop my awareness from my mental plane, thoughts, logic, and reason, and move my awareness to my womb and cervix. From here, a new dimension opens up. Silence, intuition, faith, magnetism, and well, duh, surrender. I can do this literally anywhere and in front of anyone because it has nothing to do with a person, place, or circumstance. Once I'm here, I can manifest from the raw materials of the quantum, versus the dense plane of my mind.

I see people get into all kinds of arguments about surrender and submitting on the internet. I don't think most of these people have any clue to what surrender actually means or how it feels in your body once activated. Just like faith, anyone, anywhere can surrender by letting go of control and observing their thoughts instead of taking orders from them.

Surrender Exercise/Prayer:

Today, find moments in your day to say the surrender prayer. Say it when you feel overwhelmed, worried, anxious, or just need an extra boost.

"Dear God | Universe | Angels, I surrender to you all my problems, worries, fears, and ask for guidance. Please show me how

to release all fears and embody love today. I hand over this problem to you. I am willing to do my part, please show me the way. Thank You."

Pleasure

The biggest difference, in my opinion, between a woman and a feminine woman is pleasure. Pleasure can't be faked. You are either over-flowing in it or depleted from it. Men have a heightened radar for pleasure detectors in women. The modern day woman living in a mostly masculine obsessed culture has forgotten how to activate sensual pleasure in her body, mind, and energy.

Pleasure is a great portal into your feminine embodiment. This is something I teach deeply in my Hypnotic Sex course. Pleasure isn't something to only bring to the bedroom. You won't even make it to the bedroom if you don't already have pleasure in your body.

Make pleasure a default of how you live your life. Bring it to your everyday actions, relationships, business, money, and even the smallest daily experiences and events. It almost feels like I had two lives, the one before pleasure and the one after. Pleasure activated a whole different paradigm for me. It is such a deeply feminine trait and quality. Worth taking the time to master. A woman full of pleasure in her body magnetizes not only men, but also money and magic into her reality.

Daily Pleasure Practice

Train yourself to use all of your five senses at the same time. Start with noticing all of your five senses when eating, taking a walk in nature, and taking a bath or shower. If this is too difficult, start with noticing only one sense at a time and then add another one and another one until you gain the skill to use all five at the same time. We can 10X the amount of pleasure we feel when we become aware of our body and how the environment interacts with it. This exercise may feel strange in the beginning. Your brain may even trick you into thinking you are not "getting it" or "it's too hard," but I want you to keep practicing. Trust me it's worth it.

For the second layer of your pleasure practice, do at least one thing every day for the sheer pleasure of it. No other outcome is required. This can be especially difficult for stage two Self-Aware Barbies who have trained themselves to only do things that are practical and have a very specific outcome. Pleasure is a worthy outcome.

Intuition

"*How do you make decisions so quickly? Aren't you afraid of making the wrong choice?*" I get asked some version of this question almost daily from my students who see me making massive, paradigm shifting moves on the daily.

Here's the thing, love, I don't believe in bad decisions. Failure doesn't exist in my vocabulary. What if every decision you made was the right decision? And even if you did make a wrong move, the Universe simply rerouted you, picking up any lessons or activations you needed to learn along the way. This is how I have seen my life unfold.

The reason I move fast is because I trust my intuition. Your intuition is your relationship with your metaphysical self. When we are overly identified as "our human self," decisions are hard. We must weigh the cons and pros of every decision, ask our clueless friends and family members for permission, and then run the entire process through our limiting beliefs until we are paralyzed through analysis paralysis.

There is another way and it's way more efficient and faster. Tap into your intuition, your internal knowing and universal guidance system. Intuition is not a mental process. It's a full body, sensory, energetic, and accessing the field type of process. It's quite hard to even understand or explain logically. The most brilliant people to have walked the planet tapped into this divine computer of infinite intelligence.

If you have started doing the pleasure sensory practice I shared in the previous section, you are halfway there. Just like the most pleasurable experiences of eating food, or walking in nature, or romance is not a single sense process, neither is intuition. You don't just taste your food. You experience it through sight, smell, sounds, touch, and taste. In my SAB days I would inhale my food without any conscious awareness of any of these senses. The SAB works on instincts not intuition.

By becoming aware and using all of your senses at the same time, you are now preparing yourself to access your intuition. Contrary to popular belief that we all have one primary way of accessing the metaphysical realm, for example through our clairaudient or clairvoyance; we actually access more of the field when we learn how to access all of our senses at the same time. Just like you get more information by taking in both verbal and nonverbal communication at the same time.

Yes, this will take practice but trust me it's worth the effort. If I only "listen" for my intuition, I may miss the textures and tastes that accompanied the sounds to create the full download. People who believe they are one claire or another have just trained themselves to dominantly use one sense over the others and can be missing important aspects of their intuition. Don't make this mistake.

Here is a simple Intuition Exercise to get your started:

Take a couple of deep breaths and get into a relaxed state. Ask your intuition a simple question. Nothing too complicated or layered to start with. I started with, "*What color should I wear today?*" And then drop any expectation of HOW the answer will be delivered to you. Get silent and the answer will come in a split internal knowing through one or the combination of senses.

Don't overthink this process. It's not a mental exercise. If nothing comes through, try again later with a different question. These things often take practice to unlock so never get disheartened if it doesn't work the first time around. You are creating a relationship with your intuition and like any relationship, it can take time to build trust and respect.

Truth Testing

Another layer of intuition is truth testing. Truth testing is the intersection of your desires and your intuition. Think of it as what you desire and what is the fastest route there.

There are three different methods of truth testing that I love. You can use any one or a combination of the three.

Truth Testing Option One: Leaning Into and Away From

Stand or sit with an upright posture. First test your poles by making sure your aligned to Yes is leaning forward and No is falling backward. You can test this by asking yourself factual questions like, "*My name is Mina*" and then see if it works the way it should.

If your poles are reversed then tap your right hand to your left arm and your left hand to your right arm 3-4 times, this forms an X in front of your chest will help reverse the poles back in alignment.

Then you can test it out again and resume truth testing.

Truth Testing Option Two: Pendulum Testing

Use a pendulum to truth test. You can buy one or create one by using a necklace with a pendant. The first step is to train the pendulum to give you a YES or a NO in a certain way.

For example, I have trained mine to circle around for yes, move side to side for no, and move back and forth to say, "*Ask a different question.*"

You train it by saying, "*This means Yes*" while manually moving it in the way you want it to move for yes. And so on.

Truth Testing Option Three: Truth or Lie

Think of something you really truly love. Don't choose a person or thing that you have a love hate relationship with since then this method won't work properly.

Close your eyes and place your hand on your heart as you hold the image of the thing you love in your mind's eye, visualizing it in front of you. Repeat, "*I love you*" to this thing and notice how you feel in your body. Most people report feeling expansive, light, and happy as they send love to this thing they love!

After about a minute, open your eyes and remove your hand from your heart. Do something else for a couple of minutes and then close your eyes again, placing your hand on your heart. Now put the image of the thing you love back in my mind's eye, visualizing it in front of you. This time say, "*I hate you*" to this thing you actually love. Essentially lying. Do this for a minute while noting how you feel in your body when a lie is told.

Notice how different a lie feels in your body compared to a truth!! This exercise changed my life in so many ways. I can now tell not only if I am lying to myself or if someone else or something else is not in agreement or resonance with me.

An Important Word on Truth Testing

Truth testing is not a one and done type of process. Unfortunately, most of us are not that advanced in our inner work to read the metaphysical realm in one go. We are only able to receive information from the frequencies we are currently tapping into. So, when you truth test in a state of confusion or duplicity, you may get more confusion or duplicity back.

The best thing to do is to track your truth over time. What this looks like for me is to ask the same question at different times of day, and for many days straight. Also track not just what answer comes through, but how you feel minutes and even hours and days after the answer.

Here is a recent example from my life. Most of my current examples revolve around shopping at Chanel so bear with me. I was recently at Chanel looking at their 23A collection release. My sales agent brought out the most gorgeous mermaid blue sequin flap bag. I literally gasped when I laid eyes on it! It was so stunning!

I truth tested the bag immediately when the SA handed it to me. *"Should I purchase this bag?"* It was definitely a "*hell yes!*" I asked her if she had any more in stock. She informed me that they had just received shipment only moments ago and had three in stock. I asked her to bring them all out for me to inspect and choose the best one.

I put the one I had already tested back on the counter and tested bag number two. I got an immediate "no" so I handed it back to her. I then truth tested bag number three. This bag gave me a "yes" and then suddenly I started feeling really bad in my body. Now most people would be really confused by this reading. But you see, the Universal field of intelligence communicates in frequencies and therefore there is a communication barrier between us and it. This is why tracking the truth is so important beyond the initial yes or no answer.

What the field was saying about the third bag was this, "*You will be really happy buying this bag now, but something about this purchase will make you unhappy later.*" I handed this bag back and checked out with the first bag. In which I had a consistent yes.

Please note that your frequencies, mental, and emotional states interfere with the truth testing process. If you have a lot of limiting beliefs around a certain answer, that will give you conflicting results. The best results come when we are truly neutral. Truth testing is a skill set that will improve over time. So, keep practicing!

CHAPTER *Nine* WHEN GOD IS YOUR BUSINESS PARTNER

"*I prayed and you showed up saying exactly what I needed to hear.*" "*Do you have cameras inside my head, it's like you know exactly what I am thinking, right when I am thinking it.*" These are the two most common comments underneath my YouTube videos. I believe the needs and desires of my people speak to me through my desires. The experience is of waking up with this unshakable desire to post a particular something. The desire is so intense, I can't not post it! And that is exactly what the right people need at the right time.

I believe most people have this ability in their work and life. However, we get so stuck in creating, doing, posting "the right things" or the things someone else has success in that we forget to tap into this divine intelligence. When I first started my YouTube channel in January of 2011, I found myself falling into this trap. Wanting to post what I thought would be seen by more people or possibly even go viral.

However, making that sort of "should content" never felt satisfying. Following my heart has never done me wrong. The only true instructions you need in your life and business, as cliche as it may sound, is to truly drop in and follow even the most crazy desires of your heart. Even if they don't make sense at the time. God always has a bigger plan for you and your work.

Real Desires always feel exciting and expansive, even when they scare us! "Shoulds" feel blah or downright wrong and cause a lot of analysis, logical back and forth, and even comparison cons and pros list which further confuse us.

Being a heart-centered entrepreneur truly requires you to use both your left brain and right brain and heart and mind in co-creation and divine collaboration. You are going to have to break your addiction to only using the logical side of your brain. The feminine and masculine must work together in divine union in your life and business.

There is no feminine without the masculine. To truly be in flow in your creativity as an entrepreneur or even in your career or life, you need the structures of your masculine. On a personal level, my daily routines and habits are the masculine structures that allow me to feel safe enough to drop into my flow on a daily basis.

The Masculine Containers in Business

The masculine in your business are the systems, structures, and procedures. The brick and mortar building in which you conduct your business, the website, the payment processing systems, the social media platforms are all examples of the masculine containers that hold your business together. Without these structures you are simply a starving artist. There would be no real way for people to find your work or feel safe paying you.

The masculine containers in your business not only allow automation and a sense of safety for you and your clients, they allow you to drop into flow and actually share your skillset and artform. Without this predictable automation, you would appear like a hobby to the world instead of someone to take seriously as a master of their craft.

In my business, my YouTube channel, website, and Thinkific platform where we host our digital courses are my masculine containers. When you land on one of my YouTube videos and click on a course link, there is a very predictable buyer's journey that follows. You are taken to a sales page, with a very clear and easy to see checkout button. Upon checking out, the course immediately appears in your student dashboard. All of this is the beautiful providing, protecting, and containment of the Divine Masculine at play.

If you remove this masculine system, I'm just another starving artist making content on the internet. The biggest difference between those that are successful in their business and career and those that aren't are how they are using both their masculine and feminine polarities.

Master Your Craft

You may be wondering at this point where and how does the feminine show up in your business? The feminine in any business is your skillset, craft, or talent. It's the art you create through the mastery of your craft. For the surgeon, the actual surgery is the feminine. It's the masterful art of the doctor, meticulously executed in flow. It's the divine moving through her and enhancing and using her in miraculous and magical ways.

I believe we are all born with several of these God-given gifts already pre-programed in us. They must, however, be enhanced through practice and mastery in our life. That is the art we create. Please do not take mastery to mean perfection. Art, as is life, is quite messy at times. You + Divine = Art. Universal intelligence interacting with your intelligence creates your craft. Both are necessary ingredients to the magic you create.

In my personal journey, I have made it a point to give this universal field of intelligence a lot to work with. Instead of studying just one subject or topic, I have studied many subjects and topics both wide and deep. It's the difference between giving the field one language versus many languages from which to translate its art. The more I learn, the more universal intelligence has to work with.

The seven years I spent deeply studying nutrition, hunter-gatherer lifestyles, and autoimmune diseases helped me enhance and master my skills in relationship coaching. Studying evolution and anthropology in university helped me understand religion and spirituality. Remember that in the Universal field, nothing is wasted. It's all used as raw materials to work with. My ability to weave together disciplines and knowledge codes that on the surface are not connected, is my divine art.

Spend time acquiring high income skillsets. As it turns out, I didn't have to figure out what was a high income skillset. My heart simply led me to it. My divine assignment was to study with passion everything God led me to. Study it deeply and study it widely. How it will eventually fit into the entire matrix of my intelligence was not my problem to worry about.

Qualify Yourself

"*You have 40 certifications!! Wow, I didn't know that many certifications even existed!*" That was my shocking response to a client's sudden revelation on our coaching call. We had been working together for a few months at this point on getting her business off the ground. She had never mentioned her 40 certifications before on our calls but suddenly it all made sense.

She was jumping from business idea to business idea. Website creation to website creation. Had even purchased over a dozen different domain names, each time claiming that this was it, she had finally decided.

"Babe, technically you are more qualified than me to be launching and running your business, but there is one key difference on why I have a business and you don't."

"*Please tell me what that is,*" she said and laughed nervously through the phone.

"*You haven't qualified yourself,*" I responded.

I see this all the time. Brilliant, kick ass, amazing women, chasing certification after certification, coach after coach, mastermind after mastermind hoping for something to suddenly help them feel more certain, more qualified, more worthy of doing the thing they are already destined and born to do.

While all of these can be expansive and helpful in their own way, an amazing coach, a new website, or that new fancy microphone isn't going to give you the qualifications you seek from outside of you. You must qualify yourself. Give yourself permission to be the master of your craft. You have to appoint yourself as the expert and then become it.

God Has already Qualified You. Have You?

So instead of waiting on that website to be created, launch now and let the website develop over time. Instead of waiting on purchasing the perfect camera before filming and starting your social media, start with your iPhone. Side note: Did you know I have made over eight-figures in my business using only my iPhone the entire time. I have no fancy equipment. And no, the cameras were not as fancy on my original iPhones when I started, but I used them anyway.

A new microphone isn't suddenly going to give you the courage to speak your truth. You have to give yourself permission to be seen and heard first. Work with what you have now, and then improve over time. That is you backing yourself up and truly creating art. Don't let the figuring out stage of something or that new purchase of the right gear stop you from making art with the Divine. I believe true creation is using what we have on hand first and upgrading later as our craft expands.

Qualifying ourselves is about deciding to be enough and the willingness to work with what you currently have. Even if we are still learning, still growing, and may not have all the perfect answers yet. There is someone out there that needs your exact flavor of intelligence delivered in exactly your unique way. Don't make them wait for it.

When Angels Do Your Marketing

I run an eight-figure brand with God, not only as my business partner but also my algorithm. My business students have often heard me say, God is my algorithm, and Angels do my marketing. I have created this success with zero dollars spent on ads. The right people always seem to find me at exactly the right time. Do I show up and do my part, hell yes! I love being the hands and feet of God. When God says jump, I never question it. I move, always in divine alignment.

Internally, the experience feels like me over here doing my thing in my little corner of the internet and then the right people coming to me if they so desire. There is no energy of pushing, chasing, or pursuing on my end. I do not NEED anything from anyone. They can simply choose to come hangout with me if they want.

In my industry, as I am sure in yours, there are a lot of rules and "shoulds." Apparently, I have broken all of those rules and still ended up more successful than I even imagined. Energy and results follow our beliefs. If we believe something is hard and can only be done in this one particular way, then you must do it that hard way to get the results you desire. I believe there are infinite potential ways of getting to the desired result. I just choose the one I am most aligned to at the moment and then reroute myself if needed later. I have trained myself to always look for an easier, more aligned way. Easier doesn't always mean easy, but it does mean changing things around to suit my needs or at the very least removing negative emotional energy and allowing the process to unfold.

Savage Money

I have always had the Midas touch when it came to manifesting money in fun ways through my various jobs and businesses. I didn't need much inner work when it came to the feminine aspects of money. The bulk of my inner work around money happened in the masculine realm. As you may recall from earlier chapters, my conditioning around masculine aspects of money was non-existence.

The feminine aspects of money revolve around our ability to manifest and fully enjoy money with ease and flow. Think of this realm as tied directly to your sacral chakra or life force energy. Money from the feminine is fun, easy, effortless, full of pleasure, and abundant. This is the stage of overflow. In our feminine, we want to turn money into fun experiences. We don't chase or pursue money in the same ways we don't chase or pursue men in relationships.

Masculine aspects of money revolve around our ability to hold and keep money. Anything to do with structures, systems, and keeping score will be the masculine realm. Budgeting, saving, investing are all necessary structures around money if we want to create wealth. My conditioning had taught me that I was bad with numbers and that saving money meant that I couldn't have fun. Money would literally burn a hole in my pocket in my twenties. Despite making multiple six figures a year in my early twenties, I rarely had anything to show for it.

Luckily, I did my masculine money inner work before starting my current business. I can't tell you how many entrepreneurs I have met who make millions a year, and one even monthly, who still live hand to mouth. Desperate for the next client or sale. The feminine without the masculine creates this starving Artist energy at every income level.

My net worth now has truly broken many generational curses. True wealth can only be created at the integration of both feminine and masculine money. I noticed that entrepreneurs, especially, have a hard time with the masculine aspects of money. While salaried people have a harder time with the feminine. Of course, this varies from person to person but it's just a pattern I have noticed. In some ways it makes sense. Entrepreneurs are creatives and artists who lean more on their feminine side in many aspects of their work. Salaried people have been conditioned to believe that money is not only limited but dependent on their job, forcing them to lean more on their masculine.

Many people miss this polarity in money. A truly wealthy person needs to not only be able to manifest money in a way they love and enjoy, but also keep it and grow it. This is a healthy relationship with money and one that is way more enjoyable and stable then overly leaning on just one energy.

Here is the deal, our core beliefs dictate what energy we bring to every aspect of our lives. My beliefs that "I am bad with numbers" would literally give me a headache every time I would sit down to read a financial literacy book or watch a video on managing money. So, I did what I know how to do best. I went to the root cause and decided to change my complete relationship with money. Once my core relationship with the feminine and masculine aspects of money was healed, it suddenly became so much easier, and even fun to become financially literate in masculine structures.

Feminine Money

Feminine money is all about the energy we bring to money. This energy is largely a result of our core beliefs around it. My personal core belief is that God will never run out and Barkat can be used and activated to my advantage at any time, helping me keep a light, fun, non restrictive energy with money. I have faith that God wants me to be prosperous. I also deeply believe in my manifestation powers because of both my human side and my metaphysical side. They work together in divine union.

I believe money is an unlimited resource and I can always choose to create more of it. Money is meant to be enjoyed in deep pleasure. Making money, spending money, and growing money is in sacred service to this planet and beyond. The world needs me to be rich. I believe all this and more for you as well. There is no way I would be able to create the impact I have created for hundreds of thousands of women if I didn't have the safety, security, and pleasure that comes from having money. The Divine Feminine gives through her overflow.

The treasure to divine riches is buried in the deepest desires of our heart. I never make, spend, or use, or think about money in any way that makes me feel bad. Money is supposed to be fun and easy. I'm not available for it being anything other than utter joy and bliss in my life.

I went to the university that I wanted to, studied only what was fun, created businesses I love, spent time expanding my skill sets in everything my heart was pulled towards, and now teach and create only what I love. All of this has compounded my divine riches and royalties.

Turns out money is magnetized to expansion just like everything else in life. Everything in existence seeks its own expansion and growth. Money is no different. People who have constricted, tight, hard, energy with money, manifest it in constricted, tight, and hard ways. People who love making money and enjoy being with it, spending it, giving it away, and living in pleasure with it, create and spend it in fun ways.

Barkat is a very feminine aspect of money as it has been discussed in a previous chapter. Where are the leaks in your Barkat when it comes to money? A leak in Barkat occurs when we "waste" money by spending it somewhere we didn't enjoy or fully appreciate. When our feminine energy around money is wounded, we tend to develop the following issues with money.

Feminine Wounding Around Money

- Addictions to spending money in ways we don't really enjoy.
- Manifesting free items only or money only through other people. Never really allowing ourselves to be the channel of money.
- Recycling old energy by getting trapped in the word of refunds and rebates.

Masculine Money

While feminine money is about the energy we bring to our relationship with money, masculine money is about the structures we create around it. How intimate are you willing to get with your numbers? Can you do it without making it overly hard and complicated? Budgeting, saving, and investing money has been overcomplicated by many. Most have no clue how to even start creating these structures and containers around money. For those that do attempt it, they admit that it can make them overly cautious and in scarcity around money.

Here is the truth: More money won't suddenly make you feel safe and secure with money. How you currently feel about money, yes, in this exact moment, will only be amplified the more you make and have. Money is a massive amplifier of energy. If you don't feel safe and abundant now, you will feel even more insecure and even less abundant the more you make and have.

Abundance and scarcity exist at every income and net worth level. In fact, I was watching an interview on YouTube yesterday of a couple who had a net worth of over four million dollars and were terrified of spending money. They talked about not being able to enjoy brunch at a casual restaurant with friends without worrying about money.

You also won't suddenly become financially literate when more money shows up. If this was the case then over 95% of lottery winners wouldn't end up broke and even in bankruptcy within five years of cashing in their winnings. All skill sets must be learned and embodied over time.

I often get asked how to create masculine structures with money without getting into low vibrations of scarcity. My formula has been to embody both the masculine and feminine energies of money at the same time. This will keep my faith high while also doing all the earthly, human things that must be understood and put into practice.

My biggest advice is that even if you have a spouse or financial advisor helping you create that masculine container around your finances, invest in becoming financially literate yourself. Financial literacy is a very high income skill set. It has helped me to journal to reset and rewire my beliefs around the following sensitive topics around money. Saving, emergency funds, spending, waste, and debt. Let's explore these topics a bit.

Masculine Wounding Around Money

- Inability to enjoy money leading to hoarding money and never really circulating it in ways we enjoy.
- Inability to save money or save at the expense of life force energy and pleasure.
- Here are some journal prompts to start your journey. You can also find a link to my Millionairess Playshop in the resources section at the end of this book.

Journal Prompts:

What was my mother's feminine relationship with money? What was her masculine relationship with money?

What was my father's feminine relationship with money? What was his masculine relationship with money?

What did I learn from both of them? How did this form my own relationship and beliefs around money?

Are my current money struggles more in the feminine manifesting realms or in the masculine keeping and having it realm?

___

___

___

What are my current core beliefs around money? Do these beliefs serve my next level relationship with money?

___

___

___

What new core beliefs do I need to embody to create a new level of money identity?

___

___

___

Go back to the chapter on core beliefs and use the 6 step system to rewire your core beliefs.

Overflow

I have remixed the concept of saving into overflow in my consciousness. Saving money never really felt good to me in my twenties. At the time, it felt like you could either save or spend. Being able to do both never occurred to me. So, I spent it because that always seemed like the more fun thing to do. Years later when I discovered the Law of Attraction, I realized saving could be just as fun as spending! Saving, or overflow, is a collection of Barkat. I love seeing the divine currency of the Angels, Barkat, going in my portfolio. Savings is simply a manifestation of Barkat.

Overflow in my life never comes at the expense of anything else. It just is a natural byproduct of your belief systems and what you decide you get to have and hold. Overflow also expands my belief that God will never run out. The Universe is not a peasant or limited in any shape or form. Even when I release overflow in large chunks, for example for charity or to pay taxes, it is so fun to see it quickly replenish based on my beliefs of how much I get to have in savings, investments and my net worth at any given time. The universal law of Barkat quickly fills the space that is created with letting something go with love and appreciation.

This may sound a bit silly, but one thing that also makes me very excited about saving is the various bank tiers and levels offered by our bank. Moving up the tiers feels like an energetic trophy to me. The services and white glove treatment ups the ante at every stage making it even more exciting to reach the next one. For some people this may create too much stress or pressure, but for me it's a fun game that I get to play.

At some point the overflow you create will become an overflow of blessings for your descendants. This is the true proof of breaking generational curses of poverty, never having enough, or having to struggle with money. Nothing makes me happier than imagining my children and grandchildren inheriting my energy, my name, legacy, intellectual assets, and estate.

Emergency Funds

"*Mina, I try to save money for my emergency fund, but then an emergency comes up and I have to use that money.*"

"*Well, you called in emergencies and even labeled your overflow after them so what's so surprising about them showing up? Why not call it a treasure fund or adventure fund?*"

Names are important. Label intentionally. The energy of a treasure fund or adventure fund or liquid riches is way more divine and high vibe than an emergency fund. Notice that it gives very different energetic instructions on how money should behave in each of those containers. What will yours be called?

I believe it is important to cultivate the art and craft of setting aside money in investment containers for our future self and even our descendants. This ability opens up portals of financial intelligence in us beyond just the actual accumulation of cash. As women, feeling safe really allows us to activate our feminine energy and money does represent that root level safety for us in this time.

As part of my advanced level inner work with money, one thing I did was remove my attachment to money from the root chakra and reroute it to my crown. I definitely had to work my way up to this as this goes against the current morphogenetic understanding of money as root level safety and security. This new way of engaging with money has helped me channel it through my spirituality and not from survival.

The Energetics of Spending

I only spend money from a high vibe place. Yes, I am that annoying person at the register that has to pause, close my eyes, and hand over my card only when I am feeling my most high! Being this intentional about circulating money has brought so much joy to my life. For one, it helps me really tap into my emotional state at the time of any purchase. It helped me realize that I shop when I am feeling safe, secure, and very happy in what I am creating and take a break from shopping when feeling a creative block. I wouldn't have realized this if I was spending without any conscious awareness.

I can't tell you how many wrong purchases this has actually prevented, especially when online shopping. Spending this way is actually a great way to save money. I noticed that if I had even one wrong item in my cart when checking out in person or online, I can't get myself in the high state I need to check out. Once I remove that misaligned item, I am suddenly able to get myself in a high state and check out.

I look at spending money as investing in myself and my vibration. Investing in myself is one thing that has never failed me. It's my highest rate of return. I outperform the market every time. Spending in this way has helped me discern between investments and impulsive purchases because the energies of the two are so vastly different.

Wasting Money

"*How about a Brazilian steakhouse?*" I suggested. Hoping my favorite style of cuisine would be selected.

"*No, we can't go there because then we will overeat.*" Said one of our friends as we were trying to decide where to go eat with our friends.

"*Well, can we go and eat a normal, comfortable amount of food and not overeat?*" I asked.

"*Well, then we would be wasting the buffet,*" our friend replied.

This is often the crazy making logic of being wasteful. You being uncomfortable because you overate as not to "waste" money is not being responsible with money! That is you being irresponsibly with your energy and your body. I get it, sometimes the food is just so good that we simply stuff ourselves silly. But to overeat so as not to waste money is just downright ridiculous.

Many of us were trained in these crazy rules in childhood. We were forced to eat things and finish things beyond our enjoyment. I have taught my children that finishing something is not necessary to enjoying it. Wasting their time and energy is not worth it! You and your energy are the most precious thing. We can simply use and enjoy things and experiences to our enjoyment level and then stop. When you invest your money in things or experiences, they bring you joy and uplift your energy, that is you using money, not wasting money. We have created such weird distortions around waste. We eat things we don't like, and consume things we have outgrown out of guilt of wasting. This ruins our Barkat!

Now that I have truly proved to myself and the world that my energy is literally worth millions of dollars, people suddenly respect me for honoring and protecting myself even if I "waste things" based on society's standards. I really wished I had learned to honor and back myself up in this way earlier in life. I have bought books that I only read half way because anymore would be wasting my time and energy. I rather "waste" money on a book half read than my precious time and energetic resources. I believe that I got all that was intended for me from that purchase.

People who waste their time, life force energy, and vibration in the hopes of not wasting money, have no idea how money actually works. Don't let them guilt you into finishing things past the enjoyment expiration.

Years ago, I was once led to a three-hour talk. I watched the first 20 minutes and loved it but couldn't get myself to watch anymore. Feeling guilty because I had paid for it, I came back the next day to force myself to watch the rest of it. Only to find out there was nothing more of value in that training for me. My intuition had led me away from it after I had gotten exactly what I needed, which was more than worth what I had paid for.

Sometimes the decision to purchase something or show up somewhere is the only thing we need to experience or learn from that transaction. All transactions are energetic exchanges. The transmission happens instantly, there should be no force or coercion required. This means you don't always have to "finish" the thing to get something out of it.

I once ditched a $50,000 coaching package because I no longer resonated with the coach and her teachings. I don't consider this "wasting money." That experience taught me a valuable lesson that my internal guidance was the only business advice I truly needed to follow. Following someone else's "formula" wasn't what I needed. The confidence I had in my own internal GPS was priceless! I am happy to "waste" that kind of money on life changing lessons any time because they ultimately make my faith stronger.

Your energy is worth millions more than you even realize right now. Instead of worrying about wasting money, focus on enhancing your life force energy which greatly impacts your vibration and the level of wealth you are then able to call in.

Debt

Debt is borrowing from your Barkat bank. What you do with the borrowed money and your energy around it will determine how fast you are able to repay it. Most people screw this part up because of shame or guilt around borrowing money. Instead of using that borrowed energy to create a masterpiece, they go into doubt and shame.

My parents would accumulate debt, pay it off, and then accumulate debt again. Sheena once told me never to pay off debt completely since it only comes back. I don't think we need to treat debt like the boogie man. I can see why what she said would make sense according to their beliefs and reality. If your mindset is one of negativity towards debt, and your core beliefs don't change as you pay it off, it will only return back.

I see debt as the Universe backing you up before you are ready to fully back yourself up. When you see everything as an expression of love, faith, and abundance, debt can't exist in your overflow. Instead of trying to pay off debt, focus on changing the beliefs and stories you tell about it and it will lose its power over you. The emotional energy that is then freed up can be channeled into creating the type of art that brings us an overflow of blessings and abundance. That overflow will erase the debt without any extra effort on your part.

How to Eliminate Debt Once and for All

Step #1. Remove your negative emotional energy from debt by changing your core beliefs about it. Right size it in your mind. Debt isn't good or bad. Stop judging it negatively. It's just borrowed energy from Barkat. Wealthy people often use debt to their advantage. They aren't telling the same stories about debt that you are. The energy of guilt and shame creates more debt and keeps us feeling trapped.

Step #2. Since debt is borrowed energy from Barkat, it is heavily gridded with Barkat energy. Use this to your advantage. Use the debt to create something beautiful that will serve you and others from your overflow. Remember that things we create in sacred service compound Barkat.

Step #3. Use the overflow that is created from Barkat to pay off that debt.

I borrowed money to partially pay for my education at Northwestern University. Education supports Barkat as it expands us and others around us from our overflow. I never had even an ounce of regret, shame, or guilt for financing a part of my education. My education created overflow not only in my life but in the lives of millions of people who have watched my YouTube videos and taken my courses. My videos on YouTube have been viewed over 10 million times. Each person who has benefited from my work gets me Barkat credit. I now use that education in my sacred work, courses, live streams, and books. Those student loans can't exist in the overflow that is created from my use of that money.

Money is an Arbitrary Decision

I once had a friend tell me I dressed too conservatively and should turn it up in the wardrobe department for my photoshoots the same week someone on YouTube left the following comment.

"*I am unsubscribing from your channel unless you stop showing your legs.*" The comment was left under a picture I posted wearing a knee length shift dress.

I was discussing the irony of the two very different comments I received in the same week about how I dress with my husband.

"*Well, clothing is such an arbitrary line,*" he replied. "*In some cultures it's inappropriate to show even your ankles while in others you show up in what essentially looks like underwear and call it a bathing suit. What if aliens came to visit us someday and think it's really odd that we have clothing in the first place.*"

That last bit had me laughing. It's so true! Who made the ultimate decision where to draw the clothing line. Or to have clothing in the first place! Someone decided and we all went along with it.

Money is also an arbitrary line. We have culturally and also individually decided what's too much, too little, or just right. Even in your own personal journey, I bet there have been many instances where you outgrew or stretched out the money line you had created.

I was earning $7 an hour in my first job as a teenager and thought that was a lot of money. When I started life coaching, I was charging $100 an hour, which seemed like a lot of money at the time! Earlier this year I was charging $33,000 for a package of ten, 20 minute sessions. I recently turned down a $200,000 coaching package a client was offering to do some private work with me because I was appalled at how low it was priced. Money is a decision we make.

I agreed to every single money transaction I have ever had. Yes, sometimes it felt like I didn't actually have a choice, but I always did. What I allow myself to earn, save, spend, and invest grows and expands as I grow and expand. My core beliefs need to be updated as I outgrew my old money consciousness. Some people never take the time to examine and update the arbitrary lines and stories they have inherited or created about money. Our beliefs around what we get to have dictate what we ask for and allow in our relationship with money.

I love money and believe it gets to support my life journey. God has big plans for me and my life and having money is simply a natural consequence of living a divine life. Money should never be the reason that me or my family doesn't have access to a need or experience. I don't ask money for permission, I give myself permission to say yes to all my desires. Even before I was a multi-millionaire, I noticed that money showed up only after I made the decision to say "YES". If I had asked money for permission, it wouldn't have shown up.

Now that I know that money is an arbitrary line and keeps changing for me as I grow and expand, I try to normalize the next level of spending, overflow, and Barkat in the present moment even before it actually arrives. This way I speed up the process of manifestation. For example, if something seems "too much to spend on this item or experience," I immediately remind myself that in three months' time this same price will feel just the normal amount we spend in this area. This prevents any doubts or self-sabotage that may delay my growth.

The truth is I find comical what I used to consider "a lot of money" even a year ago. Not only have I normalized those amounts but I have long outgrown them. So, if I am going to outgrow those "lines" in the future, why not outgrow them now by normalizing it in the present.

Inner work prompts:

Make a list of all of your current beliefs around money. These are things that you have picked up from parents, siblings, friends, family, teachers, peers, society, and culture. Some are serving you and others not so much.

Now take a moment to look at them. Right there in black and white. Innocently staring back at you. These are your current belief systems. Which of these would you intentionally choose for yourself? Those are the ones you get to keep. For the ones that feel icky - let's work through them. Are they ultimate, absolute truths? Are they true for everyone on the planet? Are they things that the highest most loving cosmic forces would want for you?

Rewrite them into NEW, Upgraded, Core Beliefs. These will be your NEW beliefs that you will affirm thousands of times a day with high emotional states until they become a part of your genetic makeup. Every part of your cell. These beliefs should be oozing out of your pores, as every part of you celebrates and affirms this new way of thinking, feeling, and being!

Don't Negotiate with Peasants

"*There is a huge scratch on this vase,*" said a customer as she came up to the register, showing me a nonexistent scratch.

"*I'm sorry ma'am, would you like me to help find you another one?*" I replied, unsure why she brought the vase all the way to the register. I was 17 and this was only my second week on the job. My manager had assigned me to the register from the second day.

"*No, I would like a discount on this, call your manager,*" she replied.

I called the manager but couldn't wrap my brain around the situation. Why would she want to buy something scratched?

I got the answer years later in my real estate business. The clients who would complain the most about a property, finding tons of faults, would later place a low ball offer. They actually loved the place, but wanted to devalue it to bring it down to their level. I could spot this a mile away as I evolved my sales skills.

Some people will want you so badly, they will try to devalue you to be able to afford you. Ahem, I see this in relationships as well! Instead of raising their own standards, people in peasant consciousness will try and bring you down to theirs. They do this by pointing out your faults, flaws, or some otherwise imaginary scratch in the hopes that they can score a discount with you.

In my business, we have a company policy. We don't negotiate with peasants. If someone tries to discount my work in hopes of scoring it cheaper, we talk them out of buying from us. My courses are for women who know how to back themselves up, own their desires, and manifest the resources accordingly. My prices are what my prices are. And they are always rising to match my continued growth, expansion, and depth of embodiment.

I recommend you shouldn't negotiate with peasants either. People who need to find imaginary scratches to be able to afford your work or be in your energy will find faults even if you did discount yourself for them. They also in general make difficult clients to work with. Hold the luxurious energy of your value. Let that be an invitation for them to raise up their manifestation game.

We had a woman email us once after signing up for one of our courses. She kept complaining about the amazing first session live we had just had. The 600 other students couldn't stop raving about the lesson. This woman was hoping we would give her a refund but she was insisting on wanting to stay in the course. So, she basically wanted the course for free. No thank you.

Side note: The energy of refunds is such old stagnant energy. This is not a manifestation as some people seem to think. You reusing the same used up energy over and over again is not conducive to your growth and expansive. You are worthy of attracting more riches without having to cycle that same stagnant energy. Use the time and energy placed in coming up with discount and refund schemes to create and compound actual wealth. Evolve out of peasant consciousness.

Remember: For every person looking for the cheapest price, there are ten that won't hire you because you are priced too low. That is a fact! Hold the image of the people in your field being fully capable and willing to back themselves up and manifest the funds for what they truly desire.

Homework:

Go and raise your prices.

CHAPTER *Ten*
LADY BALLS, FEMININE POWER

"*Mina, you have created massive success for yourself, what is the most important part of your journey?*" I was asked this question by an aspiring entrepreneur.

"*The person I have become.*" Without hesitation the previous words spilled out. I was hearing the answer for the first time as well.

Outside success is amazingly satisfying, but it still largely lives outside of you and perhaps feels like something you can suddenly lose one day. The person you have become is something you own. That person is not separate from success.

I define success as inner peace, contentment, and abundance in the areas most important to someone. There are areas of life where I don't care for success because those areas are of little to no importance to me. As I look back on my journey with a drone view, I can't help but notice the following things: I had a laser sharp focus on the things that truly mattered and wasn't willing to settle for anything less.

This isn't always the easiest feat to accomplish in what is now considered the most distracted generation of all time. Having it all doesn't have to look like a chicken with its head cut off running in all crazy directions. It means the willingness to be brutally honest with yourself about your priorities and be willing to let everything else drop.

The wildly successful life I now live is the result of the union between my Eastern and Western upbringing. I have had the pleasure of taking the best from both cultures and leaving the noise. From my western culture, I have learned to be independent, set healthy boundaries, and have a strong work ethic. From my eastern side, I have learned to value interdependence, traditions, and relationships. Adding this all up has created a harmonious lifestyle where I truly do get to have it all. My all.

Feminine Power

Always remember that you are a woman and in a female body. Honor and respect the inner and outer workings of this divine gift you have been given. God had a plan for you when you manifested in exactly this way. I spent my teens and early 20s trying to live like a man and it was utterly exhausting. Reclaiming my femininity is what activated my wildly successful life.

In a recent conversation with a woman I met online, I found myself really confused when she kept calling me "Bruh." A little embarrassed that I didn't know what this meant, I called for my sons to see if they knew.

"*Mom, it's short for brother.*" What in the literal fuck, I thought. Then I started noticing it online everywhere! My eyes could not unsee this monstrosity. Women calling each other "brother?" What in the world is happening to society.

We are now not only expected to think, live, speak, work, and even dress like men, apparently, we are also each other's "bruhs." Please help me make this stop. No wonder both men and women have lost their grounding in this world. We have no idea who we are and what our roles are. Is the world having an identity crisis?

In the west, women try to bring equal value to a man. Dollar for dollar and effort for effort, however, increasingly feeling like we are falling short and yet so burned out. In the east, women have traditionally brought nurturing, femininity, warmth, guidance, and emotional safety among many things. This is now rapidly changing as well.

I believe we have lost our way in shiny object syndrome. Men never really have had it as good as we imagined or have been led to believe. They have put aside their own needs and feelings in service of women and children and risked their lives for millions of years. This is not something women are physically, mentally, and hormonally equipped to do.

My husband says he considers a woman trying to live like a man a downgrade for women. Men have traditionally placed women on a pedestal and taken care of their needs by putting aside their own.

Male power comes from their outward strength as a result of 15 folds more testosterone circulating through their systems than women and children. The lifestyle western culture now expects all of us to live is something even men can barely survive. Feminine power comes from her inner strength, resilience, and range. Feminine Power is solid on the inside and soft on the outside.

We will not activate our full power by trying to win at masculine accolades. Sure, your masculine energy may get an ego boost in the moment but internally there will always be an emptiness until your feminine is also fed. The things that feed the feminine have been deemed wrong, too hard, or too oppressive by modern day society. Romantic love, marriage, children, and family have all been shunned as undesirable lifestyles for women. Women are now rejecting the very things that make us happy, fulfilled, and powerful.

I found my power in my femininity, my softness, the honoring of my feminine desires, and most of all, in the love and safety of the beautiful family I have created. I have plenty of masculine accolades of success as well. And let me tell you that there is nothing compared to the love of a family. Surrender, faith, love, children, family life does not oppress me, it amplifies my life and journey in ways few words can explain.

In today's climate, having the lady balls to fight for femininity and family is the modern woman's power. I encourage you to push back the distorted messages we receive of the weakness of femininity and the "dangers" of creating a family unit. Men and women have been succeeding in monogamous relationships for 3.5 million years. We have evolved to thrive in long term relationships.

Feminine Intelligence

Studies done and documented in the book *The Weirdest People in the World* by Joseph Henrich argues that western people have developed to have a very different set of values and attributes than their eastern counterparts. This book really validated my experience going back and forth between the US and Pakistan and curious on why people behaved and felt so different in both of my beloved cultures. Western cultures have developed to value individualism, success, and prosperity over relationships.

In short, our natural tendencies in western cultures are the exact things that make relationships harder and more complicated. Eastern cultures are wired for the values and skill sets that put relationships at the center of their lives. I believe in learning whatever I can, wherever I can and this is simply fascinating to me.

When we over optimize our lives to more masculine ways of success, we lose the neural pathways that help us succeed in relationships and vice versa. The truth is that your brain is plastic. You can wire yourself to have both success in your career and relationships! I have activated this in my life by cultivating both my masculine and feminine parts. Having helped tens of thousands of successful women also do this proves anyone can have it all!

This research also helped me understand why my parents felt so inclined to help their extended family members all those years. It was their way of staying connected to their roots and families when being thousands of miles away. They couldn't fathom not sharing with the people they loved so much. I do believe there is a way to offer support without risking your own family and health and they certainly needed better ways of giving from overflow, however I get it now.

Our Feminine Brain when wired for relationships:

- Values collaboration over competition.
- Values interdependence over independence.
- Values cooperation, sharing, and relationship roles.
- Derives happiness by receiving and giving in relationships.

What the Feminine Brings to the Table

The masculine and feminine bring reciprocal values to the union. Think of it as two sides of the same coin, together they make one. Our natural feminine tendencies are one towards softness, warmth, feminine nurturing, emotional attunement, and guidance. We are the soft places for men and children to land.

We are home. Without the feminine, there is no home to put the proverbial table to.

We now have several generations of women walking around calling themselves the table, or inciting ego from men by claiming to bring their appetite and nothing else. This behavior makes not only a fool of them but a mockery of the divine, sacred relationship between the masculine and feminine. Then they wonder why men won't provide for them.

As a feminine woman, you bring your feminine presence to your home. You set the energetic stage and culture of your household. You bring the ability to give and nurture life. Your life-giving support extends also to your husband and extended family. The softness of your body, voice, tone, and words soothe even the roughest days for your loved one.

You are the one your children and husband call for both physical and emotional boo-boos. "*I want my mommy*" is every child's cry at the first sign of distress, danger, or hurt. You are the goddess that makes life worthy for humanity. You ease suffering and put a smile on the toughest of days, weeks, or seasons.

Go Slow to Go Fast

In doing this work, remember that embodiment takes time. Being an impatient person myself, I understand how hard this can be to hear. As much as I love quantum leaping and going at the speed of light, here is what I have learned. If you are starting out in the Self-Aware Barbie stage, the slower you go with your inner work, the faster you will evolve. It's the difference between spiritual bypassing your inner work and then self-sabotaging, or actually taking the time to embody something.

If you cheated on your driving exam, that would not help you drive better later. In fact, you would feel massively insecure about your driving abilities. If you instead took the time to learn to drive properly, your skills and confidence would compound over time. Embodiment of inner work is sort of the same.

Assume Everyone is Addicted to Suffering

Remove emotion out of it and understand human psychology with this one concept. We have evolved to be addicted to suffering. Overcoming this requires ninja-like awareness and the time, energy, and resources to do inner work. Most people don't have the means or the self-awareness to do this level of inner work. So, your job is to proceed with both love and caution.

Love people but keep your emotional distance when it comes to maintaining your goals and focus. That is the cold, hard truth to creating success as a modern day woman in today's anti-feminine and anti-family climate. The world will try to guilt you, shame you, and bring you down in colorful and interesting ways. Don't let their virus of suffering infect you.

The truth is that success causes amnesia anyways. Yup, when you are happy, thriving, and successful, they will forget one day and claim to have supported you all along. Your assignment is to keep your eye on the prize. That is YOU. Few people will come ask you how you are doing and genuinely mean it, but everyone will come see the chaos of your life when it is in shambles.

Focus on creating a beautiful life experience for yourself. They will either be inspired or jealous later but that is not your problem or even your business. If I am being 100% brutally honest with you, the biggest obstacles I have found on this journey were other people! It was the crabs in a bucket scenario! When crabs are placed in a bucket together, they pull each other back down when one is trying to escape! As women we are deeply wired to want to tend and befriend and never upset others. I had to overcome millions of years of programming. My solution has been to keep my inner circle of humans really tight and close, and love everyone else from an emotional distance.

Get Over Yourself

Yes, you have issues, as does every other human on this planet. You can either get lost in your drama, stories, and problems, or you can get laser sharp focus on enjoying this life and creating something of deep meaning. Make a vow to stop talking about your problems unless you are in a coaching call and in solution consciousness. Solution consciousness is where your sole focus is resolution and moving forward.

Stop hanging out with people who discuss problems, love their issues, and their entire existence is about who did what and to whom. They are brilliant, fully capable souls trapped in addicted to suffering, human bodies. Let your embodiment be the inspiration they need to snap out of it and keep it moving.

Decide Fast and then Execute with Divine Precision

When I make a decision, I become obsessed. Everyone knows it's happening so you can either come with me or get out of the way. A decision isn't a negotiation. It's not a place for seeking validation, permission, or confirmation. It's a contract with the Divine. It has been sealed and delivered.

I don't believe in wrong decisions. I decide based on my desires and move towards them, giving the Universe a chance to reroute me along the way if adjustments need to be made.

If all roads lead to you winning, then which road is the most fun to choose right now?

When I know God is on board, the stakes are high but the path is guided. You never have to do it alone. Doing it alone is a decision that you probably made at some point, automated, and forgot to update. You get to be divinely supported on this journey.

The minute I accept the assignment revealed to me as a desire, I surrender and wait for the instructions. I move my hands and feet in the direction I am shown as the next steps even if they don't make sense to my logical brain. Even if everyone else doubts me or thinks I'm nuts. I have already accepted that I am crazy obsessed when it comes to my life.

Your job at this point is to listen to the internal nudges or outside signs, and keep moving. Take the aligned action and stop doubting yourself or God.

Expand those Containers and Become a Work of Divine Art

If you are doing this right, the edges of your "container" or what you feel comfortable allowing and receiving in your reality will need to be expanded at least every three to four months. A "too tight" container will start to suffocate you. Expansion of our container requires inner work. The feminine part is working in the metaphysical by rewiring your core beliefs. The masculine part will require you to take action by removing emotion out of it and staying focused.

Your movements don't need to be huge to be impactful. It's the small steps with intention and faith that compound into huge results. This is the part that most people miss as they try to make huge changes all at once and their container explodes and self-sabotage wins.

The experience of handing myself over to the Divine to create art with has been one exhilarating journey. I can't wait to see where my desires and co-creation lead me next.

I hope the stories, journal prompts, and exercises in this book have served you well. Hopefully you are now getting in touch with your heart's desires, feminine embodiment, and feeling more confident in following those divine nudges.

The beautiful thing with art is that there is no wrong or right, no rules, or shoulds. Art just is. A creation of the most high, created in its own image.

May you become your own masterpiece.

And so it is.

Oceans of love,

Mina Irfan

ADDITIONAL RESOURCES

Mina Irfan has over 60 digital courses available on her website at www.theuniverseguru.com in topics ranging from inner work, personal power, dating, relationships, parenting, health, and wealth.

She is also the Author of **Contained in Love: Reclaiming Your Feminine Power as a Wife and Mother.**

You can find the Millionairess Playshop mentioned in the money chapter here.

To start your inner work, consider the Basic Babe Bundle here.

ABOUT THE AUTHOR

Mina Irfan is a world-renowned Author, Course Creator, Thought Leader, Life Coach, & Spiritual Mentor for High Performance, High Achieving Women looking to reconnect with their femininity. Her teachings are a combination of spiritual energy work plus her studies of Communications, Anthropology, and Evolutionary Psychology from Northwestern University. Thousands of women have been transformed through Mina's Personal Development, Inner Work, and SELF ACTUALIZATION content. Her digital courses have enrolled women from over a hundred countries representing CEO's, scientists, celebrities, famous influencers, doctors, to powerful stay at home moms and students looking to upgrade their quality of life through inner work.

Mina Irfan stands for female empowerment through Inner work, Personal Responsibility, and Activating your Authentic Divine Feminine Power. She lives with her husband and 3 kids in Houston, Texas.

Mina can be found on www.theuniverseguru.com

YouTube channel: www.youtube.com/theuniverseguru

Instagram: @theuniverseguru_lifestyle

TikTok: @mina_theuniverseguru

ACKNOWLEDGEMENTS

My deepest gratitude to my husband and children for their unlimited support throughout the creation of this book and all my projects. To my assistant, Henrietta Biró, for her endless support, edits, and the many back and forth with the bouncing off of ideas. My dear friend, Shahrzad Parandeh for her continued love and support over the years, for writing the foreword of this book, and being the first to read and offer feedback.

And to all the wonderful ladies in the Channeled Course and book club for their encouragement, loving guidance, and positive energy towards this book.

And for you: without you asking for this book, it would have never been co-created.

Printed in Great Britain
by Amazon

31390236R00155